<hr>

Wicca Moon Magic

<hr>

The Secret Lore Of Harnessing The Lunar
Energy To Get What You Want

–

Including More Than 33 Lunar Spells And
Rituals

<hr>

Arin Corvinus

<hr>

Table Of Contents:

Wicca Moon Magic:
The Secret Lore Of Harnessing The Lunar Energy
To Get What You Want

Copyright © 2019 by Arin Corvinus

Introduction

The Moon has endlessly fascinated people for ages—even in ancient times, people looked up to the sky, basking in her glow and absorbing her energy. They noted how everything seemed to move around her cycles, with everything from the animals' migratory patterns to the flow of the water, seeming to be related to the passing of the Moon above them. Even when they had no idea what that giant glowing orb in the sky was, they knew that she was something to be respected and revered, recognizing her innate power over the whole world.

Wiccans, in particular, have always felt a close bond to the Moon—she represents our Goddess, who is locked into an endless cycle of birth, maturation, motherhood, and finally, aging and death, month after month. She starts out on the New Moon as the Infant, aging to the Maiden around the Quarter Moon, eventually swelling into Motherhood at the time of the Full Moon, and then, once she has expelled her energy into the world, she begins to age once more, becoming the Crone before finally fading away and disappearing into the Dark Moon once more.

This cycle, this birth, maturity, reproduction, and death cycle is intimately familiar to humans in general—we are entirely in-tune with the idea that our demise is hanging over us at some point, and because of that, we oftentimes get caught up in the fear and anxiety. This is where Wicca magic can come into play.

As you develop a connection with the Moon, really learning from her passage through the sky, you find that you accept this cycle—you know that all you can do is live in the moment, and that life goes on. Even after death, even if there is no afterlife or reincarnation itself, you will find yourself redistributed into the Earth. You will decompose, nourish bacteria, which nourish slightly larger organisms, and so on until you once again reach the top of the food chain. Your energy becomes recycled, as we know that energy can neither be created nor destroyed—it simply flows on endlessly. Just as the Goddess finds herself locked into a cycle of birth and death, we find ourselves in something similar.

However, there is more to it than just that—we are able to tap into the energy of the Moon, basking in her beauty and brilliance and absorbing that magical energy to utilize for ourselves.

I remember being a young child, maybe 3 or 4 years old, watching my mother meticulously place her shallow crystal dish of water out into the light of the Full Moon. I asked her what she was doing, and she pulled me closer, telling me about how the Moon's light would imbue the water with energy that would help us keep our home happy and healthy. Now, as a young child, I did not understand the idea of the flow of energy or that the universe is constantly allowing for energy to flow everywhere—I knew good and bad feelings, and if Mom told me that the water in the Moonlight would be good enough to chase away those bad feelings, that was good enough for me.

That was my first real interaction with Wicca or the Moon, at least that I can remember, and it has stuck with me. I remember the awe I felt, watching the reflection of the Full Moon on a dark night shimmer off of the water's surface. I remember feeling the urge to reach in and touch it, much to Mom's chagrin. Nevertheless, it left enough of an impression that I chose to follow in Mom's footsteps, and in the footsteps of her mother before her. We choose to live our lives by the God and Goddess, honoring them and reaping the benefits from their generous provision of energy sent out into the world.

Now, not everyone is as lucky as I was and grew up so deeply in-tune with nature, the Moon, and the seasons, but this book is here to help you. As you read through this book, I will walk you through any pertinent information—teaching you everything that you need to know about the Moon and the Goddess in order to begin harnessing her energy. This can be your stepping-stone into the Wicca way of life if you desire it to be, or it can serve as a foundation to answer any questions you may have about this lifestyle that so many people choose to live.

Now, as you read this book, you will be guided through the basic foundations of Wicca magic, the Lunar Cycle, and so much more. Good luck on your journey, and thank you for joining me on this endeavor.

Chapter 1: Mankind And The Magical Moon

As a child, did you ever look up at the great night sky and feel that sense of wonder—that sense that you are looking at something so much bigger than you? If you did, you are not alone—before the invention of technology, or even of writing, ancient people looked up at the night sky for information. Despite just how massive the sky is, and despite the fact that the Earth is constantly spinning, the sky brings a sort of regularity, a familiarity as it changes. These changes come and go, and ancient people noticed the waxing and waning of the moons, which came and went at different intervals throughout the year, and eventually noted just how constantly these cycles were.

The Ancient Role Of The Moon

As these cycles became noticeable, people started to interpret them. They recognized that the Moon was not just a big bright thing in the sky that brings them light some of the time—it was something more. The ancient people, who had always revered the Moon as a god, as a sort of hypnotic, magnetic force that would compel them into action, literally changing the world around them, discovered that the Moon came and went on a regular cycle. This means that the Moon was no longer just a source of mysticism, of magic, or of light—it was a calendar as well. These full moons came regularly, and just as regularly, the Moon would seem to disappear from the night sky altogether.

The Emergence Of The Lunar Calendar

As ancient humans noted the steady, reliable changes of the Moon and began to catch onto the patterns between the environment and the changes of the moon, they started using the Moon's steady length as a calendar. The lunar calendar allows people to track the months—which is derived from the word "moon" to begin with. People began to note that the rise of specific Moons would lead to the change in seasons and that certain events would happen annually, roughly 12 Moon cycles apart.

People would chart these changes and passage of time, creating notches and holes into bones, tusks, horns, and sticks, to represent the phases of the Moon and passage of time—some of these ancient calendars were dated back *32,000 years ago*. By looking at the changes in the Moon and the relationship between the Moon and certain stars, people could begin to plan for changes. Finally, they could account for annual events and predict them. They would know when summer and winter were coming—they would know when rivers would flood, or tides would rise, or when certain foods should be planted or hunted, all thanks to the calendars directly derived from the Moon's passages through the sky.

The Modern Role Of The Moon

Today, we have no need to rely on the Moon to predict the passage of time, but if you have listened to music, or even looked at a list of popular baby girl names these days, you would see its influence everywhere—people still sing songs about the mystery and magic of the Moon's light, and the name Luna is even in the top 25 names given to baby girls in the year 2018. Despite the ready availableness of calendars literally in pockets at nearly all times, however, the moon is still important.

Despite not needing the Moon as a calendar to measure the passage of time, you can still find its influence everywhere. It influences the body, behaviors, sleep patterns, and even physical health. Women's menstrual cycles often synchronize with the Moon's cycle, and it seems to influence the minds of everyone. If you have ever spoken to someone who works with people, they always tell you that the crazy comes out during the light of the full Moon. Coincidence? Not at all.

The Moon And Astrology

Some Wiccan Moon magic is tied to astrology—as the Moon makes its journey through the sky, it spends roughly two and a half days in each of the astrological signs. As the Moon passes through these signs, people find themselves influenced by its magic. When the Moon is in Taurus, for example, people tend to become more steadfast in their emotional states, influenced by the stability of Taurus. On the other hand, if the Moon were in Sagittarius, people would feel influenced by the energy of positivity and vitality of the sign.

As the Moon travels through these various signs, people tend to naturally change their behaviors, but that is not all. The energies from the signs and the Moon as it passes through can influence magic as well. The energies projected by the Moon can be conducive to certain spells, and if you were to use the full power that you could draw from the Moon, working with it instead of against it, you could strengthen the magic you are choosing to put out into the world.

For example, if you were to perform a Spell when the Moon is in Taurus, you would want to focus your efforts on those involving money and relationships. Due to the fact that Taurus is so stubborn, it tends to create energy that will have the same steadfast and constant nature as the bull itself.

Science And Wiccan Magic

Despite common belief, magic and science are not too far off. Magic does not involve the sudden creation of fiery blazes in the palms of your hand or actively turning someone else into a beast—instead, it involves influencing the world to change around you. When you are learning to use magic yourself, you are tapping into the energy of whatever you are attempting to influence. Through ritual, you are developing your own connection to the energy in the universe—or in the case of this book, primarily the moon. You can then direct that universal energy—that cosmic energy that flows within everything, to influence it.

In science, it is commonly accepted that matter is always vibrating—that until you reach the temperature of absolute zero, at which point, all particles stop moving. When using Wiccan magic, then, you are tapping into that energy. You are recognizing that you directly vibrate with both a physical and spiritual energy, particularly when practicing your magic. During a ritual, you are connecting these two energies, these vibrations, together, and redirecting them. You become a conduit for the universe's cosmic energy, and through yourself, you direct your own intentions outward into whatever form you were hoping to change it to.

Enhancing Magic Using The Moon

As you move forward in your Wiccan journey, learning to utilize your own magic, you will discover that the Moon is greatly influential. While most people do not track the Moon's cycle, it is important that practicing Wiccans make it a point to tap into that cycle, connecting with the Moon daily. You have several ways of doing this—rituals, such as the ones that will be discussed later, greeting the Moon, or even just a few moments to reflect upon it.

When you tune into the Moon's cycle, you are then able to tap into the Moon's natural energies that are dependent upon where it is within its own cycle, or which sign it is currently in. As you do this, you can start to utilize the subtleties that exist between the varying states of the Moon. This means, then, that you can start to change when you choose to engage in your own rituals, ensuring that you are always using the energies in the world around you to their fullest potentials, enhancing your own magic.

Chapter 2: Understanding The Wiccan's View

Before you delve straight into learning to utilize and master your own magic, however, you must come to understand the Wiccan way of life—looking at the views that will be driving your own usage of magic and rituals. You need to understand the significance of the Triple Goddess, of Sabbats and Esbats, and even a solid understanding of the Afterlife from a Wiccan's viewpoint. In understanding these concepts and the beliefs driving everything, you will feel closer to the magic that you are actively learning about now.

The Triple Goddess

The Triple Goddess is one of the two deities within Wiccan practices—She takes three forms based upon the Moon's cycle, changing through the three phases, Maiden, Mother, and Crone. These forms themselves are a representation of the woman's body, representing before women can bear children, during the childbearing years, and after the ability to have children have passed. This does not mean that only women of a specific age can relate to the Triple Goddess at specific times; however, men and women can relate to the Triple Goddess sat any point in time. You do not have to be a young girl to relate to the Maiden, nor do you have to be a woman past the age of childbearing to feel a resonance with the Crone.

The Maiden

The Maiden is related to the time during which the Moon moves from crescent to waxing. This point of time is recognized as the Moon growing—it develops and grows to full, much like a girl growing into womanhood.

The Maiden, then, represents life itself—she is a new life that is growing into something more, which is capable of the creation of further life itself. She represents the innocence of childhood, the confidence and intelligence necessary to row, and this phase of the Moon is a wonderful time to engage in self-discovery.

The Mother

Just as a pregnant woman, swollen with life, the Moon becomes full and round. She gives life to the world, creating everything around us. She is the most powerful of the three forms, and she is associated with life itself. She is nurturing and comforting.

The Mother is typically considered to be related to the middle of the day, almost symbolically as her position in the middle of the life cycle. She is associated with summer and the maturation of the world that is growing into adulthood, preparing to start the cycle all over again.

The Crone

The last of the three forms is the Crone—she is most closely related to the evening and night as the life cycle ends. She is wise and respected, and yet, she brings with her the association of death and the darkness of the New Moon. Despite the relationship to death, however, she brings forth the hope of rebirth as well—she is a reminder that life will cycle once more.

Understanding The Wheel Of The Year

The Wheel of the Year is little more than the Wiccan's calendar of the Earth's rotations through the seasons. It divides up the year into eight distinct festivals, spaced evenly throughout the cycle of the year. Unlike traditional calendars that are drawn out to be linear, it is important to recognize the symbolism of the wheel in Wiccan beliefs—everything follows a cycle, and the year is no different.

Sabbats

The festivals of the year are known as the Sabbats—these are important festivals marking the passage of time—they are divided into the Greater Sabbats and

Lesser Sabbats, but all are important to understand. The Greater Sabbats are important festivals that are somewhat influenced by Germanic festivals of old, and these exist somewhere between the Lesser Sabbats, roughly halfway through, though this is not a hard-and-fast rule. The Lesser Sabbats are what most people know to be solstices and equinoxes. The eight Sabbats are:

- **Samhain:** *Greater Sabbat of the Dead (November 1st)* Often considered the most important of Greater Sabbats—it is a time dedicated to the remembrance of those who have been lost.

- **Yule:** *Lesser Sabbat—winter solstice (December 20th-23rd)* Celebrated to rejoice the rebirth of the Great God—the new solstice sun.

- **Imbolc:** *Greater Sabbat (February 2nd)* Ts when people make pledges for the year, and some Wiccans use this as the festival that initiates new members.

- **Ostara:** *Lesser Sabbat—spring equinox (March 19th-22nd)* Celebrated to honor the reuniting of the Mother Goddess and newly reborn Great God.

- **Beltane:** *Greater Sabbat (May 1st)* The fire festival celebrating fertility.

- **Midsummer (Litha):** *Lesser Sabbat—summer solstice (June 19-23)* Celebrated as the turning point in summer, marking the shortening of the days.

- **Lughnasadh (Lammas):** *Greater Sabbat of the Harvest (August 1st)* The first of the autumn festivals—this festival honors the harvest.

- **Mabon:** *Lesser Sabbat—autumn equinox (September 21-24)* A ritual dedicated to giving thanks to the Earth as the season gives way to the colder months.

Esbats

Just as the Sabbats referred to the solar cycle, the Esbats honor the Moon. The Esbats, depending on the coven, celebrate either the Full or New Moon. The primary difference between the two, however, is that while the Sabbat brings forth business and needing to honor specific periods of time that mark the Wheel of the Year's turning, the Esbats are less down-to-business. They are meant to be enjoyed and are less formal and can exist for several reasons—to honor the moon, or just to get together.

Understanding The Afterlife

As can be seen in nearly every other part of the world, in which no one agrees what will happen after death, Wiccans as well cannot agree. Some believe that death is just the end—there is nothing that comes next other than our life energy being absorbed by the universe and redistributed. Of course, this is, in a sense, its own form of reincarnation. However, most of us accept that we exist to be reincarnated. Remember, everything in life is cyclical—just as the Moon and Triple Goddess go through their cycles of birth, growth, death, and rebirth, so too do we.

However, the exact method behind the afterlife and rebirth is not quite agreed upon. Some people believe that the spiritual life begins with the most simple of organisms and slowly, the soul grows and evolves over time, eventually reaching up to human life. Others believe that reincarnation is specific to humans and that humans will be reborn as humans. Others still believe that it is possible that when we choose to be reborn, we choose the life that we wish to go through next in order to reach fulfillment. Even still, others believe that we are reborn in accordance with karma, or as entirely random. Ultimately, you must make such an intimate decision for yourself. You must choose which representation of the afterlife you wish to believe in of your own volition, deciding which resonates best with you.

The Moon And The Four Essential Elements

As the Moon travels throughout the sky, it passes through several signs, and these signs themselves are associated with elements. While there are five elements for Wicca (Air, Fire, Water, Earth, and Aether), the moon travels through four of these during its cycles. Aether itself is omnipresent, existing to connect the world together.

Fire

The element of fire is representative of the same burning passion and love that you can see reflected in flames themselves. You can represent fire through burning, lighting candles, or even baking. It is represented most closely by the Zodiac signs of Aries, Leo, and Sagittarius.

Air

The element of air is representative of the mind. It focuses on intelligence, imagination, dreams, and even psychic abilities and telepathy. It is most often represented through the act of throwing items into the wind, using scents and aromatherapy, or even singing and playing music. It is perfect to utilize for Spells that relate to freedom, knowledge, psychic development, and traveling. It is associated with the Zodiac signs of Gemini, Libra, and Aquarius.

Water

Water is representative of the soul and emotions. It is considered a more feminine element and is represented through the use of water being poured onto other objects, in brewing potions, creating healing Spells, and engaging in ritual bathing. It is associated with the Zodiac signs of Cancer, Scorpio, and Pisces.

Earth

Earth is representative of the strength and stability associated with the world itself—it is stable, abundant, prosperous, and rich. When representing this element, you may bury the item you are using, using herbs or other plants foraged, or creating effigies. It is associated with the Zodiac signs of Taurus, Virgo, and Capricorn.

Chapter 3: Practical Ways To Harness The Power Of The Moon

And now it begins! You are going to start developing an understanding of how best to harness the power of the Moon.

The Five Moon Tides

Most people know about tides—you say the word, and they immediately think about the ebb and flow of water in the ocean. The ocean rises and falls daily, thanks to the influence of the Moon. However, there are several other tides as well—the Moon's influence pulls on all substances, not just the water within the ocean. Despite the fact that the Earth pulls the Moon to it, the Moon is also constantly exerting a gravitational force onto the Earth as well. It is commonly accepted that the Moon is able to pull on the elements, but it is also able to impact life itself.

When you are talking about tides, it is important to understand how they work—there are two tides every single day. These tides correspond to the Moon's location in regards to the area that is being looked at in the moment. These tides occur when the Moon is overhead and when the Moon has traveled to the opposite end of the Earth. These are not necessarily exact—the orbit is not perfectly round, nor is the Earth or Moon. However, after billions of years of orbit, it has established enough of a pattern that the Earth follows this same shift.

Ocean Tides

This is the tide that everyone thinks of—the ocean's tides push water, causing it to recede and grow depending on the time of the day. These tides are at their most extreme during the Full and New Moons, and these are known as "spring tides." When these tides occur, you will see a more drastic fluctuation in the depth of the water.

Earth Tides

Just as the ocean shifts with the orbit of the Moon, the Earth itself shifts. As the Moon rises up over the horizon, it pulls the very Earth with it, causing the surface to expand somewhere between four inches and an entire foot, just because the Moon is overhead. The gravitational force of the Moon is strong enough to move mountains, forcing the crust of the Earth to move similarly to the tide.

Fire Tides

The center of the Earth is comprised of a molten core—it is so hot that the stone that makes up the planet has melted and exists as a liquid center to the planet. This molten core moves with convection currents, with magma rising and falling based on temperature. This is what causes continental drift. And this is still unable to escape the power of the Moon's pull. The core of the Earth is just as subject to the Moon's pull as the oceans, causing ebbs and flows.

Air Tides

Our planet is surrounded by air. This is well-known—it is what allows us to breathe. The Moon is able to influence that pocket of air, causing it to change and bulge as the Moon passes it by. As the Moon lingers over any given area, its gravity forces the atmosphere beneath it to move upwards. This shift is not as subtle as the water or earth tides—the atmosphere will bulge outwards upwards of fifteen miles in some areas.

This change in atmosphere, then, influences the weather itself. Because it changes the air pressure so much, it influences the weather, and it actually has been found that most significant weather events have lined up with specific positions of the Moon itself. As the Moon enters certain positions in its orbit, it seems that it is able to cause the weather itself.

Blood Tides

While people try to reject this notion, if the Moon is capable of shifting the very core of the Earth and literally pulling the Earth's crust up, why would it be so hard to believe that it can influence blood as well? Nevertheless, there has been evidence to show that the Earth can, and does, influence the tide of blood within life itself.

The Tides And Reproduction

The Moon, particularly when full, has been linked to ovulation and breeding cycles, and women tend to menstruate the most frequently around the New Moon. Ever wonder why the Full Moon became such a romantic object? It was thanks to the fact that women ovulate around that period, peaking their sexual desire as well. It is noticeable in several species of animals beyond humans.

The Tides And Mental & Emotional Balance

Beyond just that, however, it has been found that people hemorrhage more frequently when the Moon is full, and it has had an impact on surgery. Beyond just that, there seems to be some tie between the Moon and the human mindset. People drink more, commit suicide more, become violent more often, and become mentally disturbed more often with the Full Moon. Ask any emergency room worker—they know that the Full Moon will bring far more problems than any other period in the month.

The connection between the moon and emotional wellbeing has been believed to be linked for ages. After all, look at the word lunatic—it is antiquated now, but it was originally used to describe those of unsound mind, or those who were otherwise emotionally disturbed. The word itself literally means "of the moon." Nevertheless, this notion is largely frowned upon and denied these days, despite the fact that the moon can influence everything else around it in the world. It almost seems remiss to say that it is irrelevant to human life if it can raise mountains, move oceans, and even create weather.

How To Garden By The Moon

Gardening by Moonlight may seem difficult or even unpleasant to those who would much rather be sleeping, but it actually could influence the successes of your plants growing well. By tapping into the Moon's natural cycle, you can make the chances of your plants surviving and thriving significantly better with ease. All you need to do is learn what to plant at which points in time.

Thanks to the gravitational field that is constantly being acted upon by the Sun and the Moon, water, in particular, is shifted extensively based upon the positions of both celestial bodies. Just as the tides rise up with the full moon, groundwater is pulled upwards as well. As the water rises upward through the ground, the seeds you plant are more likely to absorb that water, allowing for them to grow better.

When you choose to garden by Moonlight, you will most often consider the moon in four quarters, each of which encompasses about a week of time. These are the New Moon, Waxing Quarter Moon, Full Moon, and the Waning Quarter Moon, which of course, cycles back into the New Moon once more.

Planting in the New Moon

During this period of time, when the Moon is dark, gravity pulls water up toward the surface of the ground. As seeds that are planted absorb readily available water in the ground, they swell—this is what prepares them to grow, and they eventually burst into a sprout. Because your plants will go through the initial swelling and bursting stage with the darkness, they should poke through the soil right as the nighttime light starts to increase, thanks to the swelling Moon.

During this period of time, you should consider growing your annual crops that will bear above-ground crops, particularly those whose seeds are external. This means that you will want to take a look at lettuce and leafy greens, cruciferous vegetables such as broccoli and cauliflower, cabbages, and grains.

Planting in the Waxing Quarter Moon

During the Waxing Quarter Moon, you will not find the pull of the Moon to be as strong—its gravitational pull is less than what you would see during a Full or New Moon. Nevertheless, thanks to the extra light from the moon, leaves grow well, creating healthy plants. The best time to plant during this period is the two days prior to the Full Moon. This will give the plants the added benefit of the extra water that will be brought upward by the Full Moon.

When growing plants during the Waxing Quarter Moon, you want to plant other above-the-ground crops that will grow with their seeds inside rather than externally. For example, you may choose this period to grow tomatoes, peppers, peas and beans, melons, and squash.

Planting in the Full Moon

By planting under the light of the Full Moon, you do have one inherent benefit—you have more light to use! Nevertheless, there are plenty of plants that will thrive being planted into the Full Moon, despite the fact that energy and light levels will begin to decrease as it all peaked with the Full Moon. As already mentioned, gravitational pull does draw water higher into the soil to allow the plants to get the moisture they need. However, as the light is decreasing, this means that more of the energy needs to be drawn from the ground and roots of the plant to sustain it.

This is not a bad thing, however—because the roots need to be active, this is the perfect time to plant crops that are harvested for their roots. This is any of the root vegetables you will need—garlic, onions, carrots, and beets, for example. This is also the perfect time during which you can plant perennials or other bulb plants. It is also a good time to transplant anything that you would like to move, thanks to the emphasis on root energy.

Planting in the Waning Quarter Moon

During the Waning Quarter Moon, you will notice that both Moonlight levels and the gravitational pull from the Moon lessen. Because of this, you are usually best served to treat this period of time as a rest period rather than one to try to plant more crops. During this period of time, you should instead tend to your plants, giving them the care that they need to thrive.

This is the perfect time of the month to use for harvesting your crops that have grown successfully. Beyond that, you can also take advantage of this period of rest to fertilize and prune your plants, ensuring they are at their healthiest or transplanting them since the nights will be dark, and the plant can redirect energy toward establishing a solid root system.

Zones, Seasons, and Planting

One important factor to consider when gardening, whether in the Moonlight or by day, is zoning. When you plant your crops, you want to make sure you are considering your own climate's weather patterns. After all, you might be able to grow tomatoes throughout the winter in Florida, but if you tried leaving that tomato plant out in Montana in November or December, you would most likely wake up to a frozen plant.

Very briefly, let's go over the zones in the United States and how these will alter your growing patterns for a handful of common crops.

Region 1: Southern United States

This is the southernmost portion of the US and involves warmer climates. In these states, you can start planting much earlier, either in late winter or late autumn to see early spring crops. Try following this guide, especially in relation to the moon phases:

- **Feb 7-14:** Plant beets
- **Feb 15-Mar 1:** Plant broccoli and other cruciferous vegetables
- **Mar 17-20:** Plant peppers and tomatoes during this period of time
- **Mar 17-31:** Plant cucumbers during this time
- **Aug 1-10, Aug 27- Sept 7:** Plant carrots during this period
- **Sept 9-24:** Plant collard greens during this period

Region 2: Coastal United States

This region encompasses both the east and west coasts of the US. As you can see, these areas are just a bit further north than the Southern areas, and the dates are pushed out accordingly to accommodate for cooler spring temperatures for longer.

- **Mar 7-16:** Plant carrots

- **Mar 17-31:** Plant broccoli and collard greens

- **Apr 15-29:** Plant cucumbers, peppers, and tomatoes.

- **Aug 27-31:** Plant beets

Region 3: Northern US and Canada

Now, you are in the northernmost parts of the country, as well as the southern areas in Canada. As you can see from the dates, these are pushed out significantly compared to when you could start gardening in, say, Florida compared to northern Washington.

- **May 1-14:** Plant your beets

- **May 15-20:** Plant peppers

- **May 15-29:** Plant broccoli, collards, cucumbers, and tomatoes.

- **Jun 13-20:** Plant another round of cucumbers

- **Jun 13-28:** Plant another round of peppers

- **Jun 29-Jul 11:** Plant carrots

Positive Charging Under The New Or Full Moon

At this point, you get it: The Moon is *powerful*. How would you like to start harnessing that power for yourself? You can do so with a handful of simple steps. The Moon is powerful regardless of the phase that it is in at any given moment, and because of that, you can utilize its energy with ease. Particularly during a New or Full Moon, however, the energy emanating from the Moon is super-powered—when you use this energy, you will see the best end results.

When you want to capture this power for yourself, you will *charge* your items. Effectively, you will take the lunar energy and allow it to fill whichever items you have chosen as the vessel for the energy. In particular, when you use the Full or New Moons, you will be harnessing the optimum time that will purify and energize your items, allowing you to repel any negativity they have absorbed. By purging the negative energy, you allow for the positive energy to enter.

What Is Positive Charging?

Everything has a charge—either positive, neutral, or negative. This is the energy that is encompassed within the item, vibrating it endlessly. This energy interacts with other objects, influencing them. The items around you will pick up energy everywhere you go, absorbing it, but some of this energy is negative and harmful. This is where positive charging comes in.

When you charge your object, you will focus your own energy and intention on allowing the negativity that has been absorbed thus far to be discharged, releasing it back into the universe. This then leaves your own object cleaned out, which then makes space for the positive energy that you will welcome in. When you choose to charge an object of your own with the Moon, allowing the item to absorb the Moon's energy, you go through a simple process.

Charging Your Object

Regardless of whether you are attempting to embrace the energy from a New or Full Moon, you will go through the same steps to charging. You will want to make sure you have all of your tools—water, a candle, a bowl, salt, and whatever you will be cleansing and charging.

Start by taking your bowl and filling it up with water. Then, sprinkle salt across the top. Preferably, you should choose a natural sea salt, which is less processed than typical table salt. The salt is used for its ability to soak up and break down negative energy.

With your bowl prepared, place it outside just after sunset. This should be during a Full or New Moon for the best end result, though really, just the act of purifying your object at another period of time will still have some sort of effect. The bowl should be positioned so the Moonlight will shine on the water, or in the event of a New Moon, you should ensure that it is sitting out to absorb the lunar energy being emanated.

Now, light your candle. You can also add a sage burn into this stage if you wish to cleanse your immediate vicinity.

Pick up the items that will be cleansed—for some, this is a crystal, piece of jewelry, or clothing, but you can purify and charge anything, large or small. If it is too large, it can be left on the ground, preferably in the Moon's light. Hold up the smaller items in your hands, so they are bathed in the Moonlight and relax into a meditative state. Doing so involves you allowing yourself to focus on exactly that moment as you breathe.

One of the easiest ways to enter a meditative state, if you do not yet know, is through taking deep inhales and exhales. Try taking a deep, long inhale for five seconds through your nose and holding it for a moment before exhaling for another five seconds. During this process, allow your body to relax and focus on your breaths and your current state.

Once you are sufficiently relaxed and you feel like your mind is clear, take one last deep breath and lower your items back down to you. Then, exhale, blowing lightly over all of the items that you are attempting to purify. As you exhale, make sure that you keep your thoughts pleasant, positive, and relaxed. As you blow, you are dusting them off, so to speak, allowing you to blow away the negative energies that may have become affixed to them.

Now, close your eyes for a moment. Imagine the energy and how it flows all around you. You can feel this as you breathe, feeling the energy enter your lungs, expand, and fill your body with life. Now, imagine how that energy flows into the items that you are cleansing. Imagine the rays of the Moon, absorbing into the surface of the items. As you do this, you need to maintain focus. You can do this with some sort of affirmation or prayer, or literally just speak what you wish to attract. For example, you may say something along the lines of:

The energies of the Earth, the Moon, and the Universe, please bathe [object name here] in your positive energy, cleansing it from negativity.

Make sure that you always include a whisper of gratitude as well, thanking the universe for the energy that it sends toward you.

Place the items within the water, if they can tolerate this or are small enough to fit. If they cannot sit in water without being damaged, you can try leaving them next to the bowl, or even burying the item as well in order to get some of the Earth's stable energy along with that of the Moon.

As you are setting down your item, now is the time to state your intention. If all this is for you is a cleanse and recharge, you can ask for that. If it is something more involved, make sure you specify that as well. However, for a beginner, you will probably start small. Perhaps try saying something along the lines of, "I request that any negative energy within my object be purged and that positive energy be allowed to flow within it."

Ideally, the items should sit out overnight, if possible. If you cannot leave the items outside for some reason, you can instead leave them in a window to allow them to still absorb some of the Moon's energy.

The next morning, if all you wished to do was cleanse your item, it is done. However, if you wish to set an intention as well, continue on. You will sit outside with your items. Sit in the lotus position if you can, and set up a candle, lighting it in front of you. Take each item you are purifying and hold them in your hand, one at a time. Keeping the item in your dominant hand with your other underneath, set your intention once more. Using your voice is the most effective way to really form that intention. If you are purifying a piece of jewelry to use to bring you calmness, for example, you declare that now, or if you are asking that a certain item give you strength during moments of weaknesses, voice that request as well.

With the item in hand, take a deep breath and focus on the vibrations of the item, imagining that both the object's energy and your own are interacting and merging together, and then switch the hand in which the object rests, placing your dominant hand underneath the non-dominant hand. It should be done. Any time you need the item or object, try to feel those same vibrations once more.

Pregnancy: Birth Rate And The Full Moon

If the Full Moon is able to influence everything from the atmosphere to the flow of blood within your body, thanks to the influence it has over gravity. It also relates to ovulation and menstruation as well, with sexual desires and ovulation both peaking right around the Full Moon. However, if you have ever gone into a labor and delivery unit at a hospital, you may have heard that there is a noticeable increase in women in labor around the Full Moon.

The idea is that the gravity created by the Moon impacts the human body. Because you are made of roughly 80% water, it makes sense that the Moon would also influence childbirth, especially considering the fact that babies grow in a highly water-based environment. While the amniotic fluid is not entirely water, it is primarily comprised of water, along with the baby's urine, hormones, and other antibodies that all mix together. The Full Moon, then, creates a gravitational pull, it is believed, and that pull leads to more births during the Full Moon period.

Now, many people deny this—they say the evidence and data are too slim to necessarily be confirmed as statistically significant. Many people will deem it as little more than the lunar effect—the idea that the Moon is capable of influencing far more than it actually does. It is believed that cognitive bias is responsible for this idea—basically, people think it is true, though it is not.

However, is this really so far-fetched to believe? If the Moon has such a strong pull on blood, it seems likely that there is some real relationship between the two.

After all, people no longer consider the Moon to be linked with the weather either, though the pull of the Moon's gravity is undeniable—it is present in the tides, in the Earth, in the air itself, and even in the center of the world.

The Full Moon And Creativity

Creativity is difficult to manage- when you are creative, you are trying to make something out of nothing. This is no easy feat—so much thought goes into creating anything at all, getting the details just right. It becomes easy for your mind to cloud, especially with stress, worry, and even just thoughts in general.

However, you can tap into the Full Moon, using that relationship between yourself and the Moon to help you tap into creativity. By letting go of all of the negativity, the cloudiness of your thoughts, and your reservations, you can release them, freeing your mind and allowing for those creative juices to flow as they should be.

Releasing your reservations is quite simple—you can unlock your creativity with a simple ritual. This ritual of letting go during the Full Moon involves a handful of steps, and you can do it with relative ease.

Start first by identifying the energy that the Full Moon is emanating—remember, this can change with the signs and the month associated with that particular Moon. With the energy identified, it is time to create an intention.

Your intention is your hope for the ritual you are getting ready to complete. You should make sure that your intention is something that you know will work for you. In this case, it may be letting go of the stressors that are holding you back and holding your creative mind hostage.

Next, make sure you spend time reflecting—do you know what you want? Why do you want that creativity? How will it help you? You want to make sure your entire mind is in agreement and that you can make sure that you know what you are hoping to achieve. In doing so, you can ensure that you understand your intentions and that you are aligning your goals with the life you are living.

Now, release your intention into the world—speak it out loud if you can. This is where you state exactly what you are hoping to achieve: Perhaps something like, "I wish for clarity and focus," or whatever else it is that you need to banish any of the negativity that is preventing you from unlocking your creative potential. Allow any negative, clouding feelings, thoughts, and energy to release from you in any way possible. Dance, shake, draw, paint, sing, or do anything else necessary to eliminate the negativity.

You can follow this up with a Tarot reading if you are interested, allowing yourself to further connect with your own energy and intentions, or you can skip this step altogether and move on. With the negative energies expelled under the light of the full moon, you should find that your creative processes are free to flow once again relatively unrestricted. Now, release that creativity into the world, making it into a better place for everyone.

Ways To Tap Into Your Intuition

Intuition is a tour's ability to understand, recognize, and acknowledge guidance. For some, it comes from the gut. It is that initial reaction in which you have a certain feeling toward a specific event or person. This sense of knowing, this tiny voice in the back of your mind, is regularly quashed by logic, reasoning, and even doubts. However, that part of your mind that is capable of understanding and reading the world around you are so important to listen to. You should always trust your intuition, and despite the fact that most people choose not to, it is good for you to go through the process of doing so. When you try to develop your own intuition, there are several steps you should go through, and each will make you that much more open and primed to listen to the energies of the universe around you, heeding their warnings.

Living in the Present

Perhaps the most basic method of trusting your intuition is through living in the present. When you do this, you do not let the past weigh on your current feelings, and you do not worry about the future. Instead, you focus on the here and now—

what you can directly and easily influence around you. In doing so, you are able to hear your intuition, unencumbered by doubts, fears, anxiety, or anything else.

Ignore the Ego

Oftentimes, the intuition that is felt is not rational—it is the energy of the universe guiding you. However, the ego is usually distracting you from that energy, whispering doubt in your ears through discussing all of the reasons why you should not trust your gut reaction, especially if it does not seem to make sense at that moment. Nevertheless, allowing yourself to live intuitively, even when illogical, can be crucial to really listen to the guidance around you.

Don't be Afraid to Ask

Sometimes, the best way to get the intuitive response you need is to ask questions. Stop and ask for the guidance that you want. Just as you would not hesitate to go ask a mentor, teacher, or friend for help, you should not hesitate to ask the universe for the answers you need.

When you do this, make sure you are specific. You can try writing out the question on paper or speak your question out loud as you consider it. Usually, you want to start by asking something that is not particularly important—what do you want for dinner? Which color tie should you wear to work? And over time, you can start to ask questions that are a bit more difficult, such as wondering how you can best get the job you want. After asking your question, allow yourself to be guided to the response.

Meditation

Meditation effectively allows you to clear your mind altogether—when you meditate, you are focusing on the moment. You are making it a point to listen to your body right then, understanding your current feelings as truly as you can. You are also able to listen to the world around you, allowing you to tap into that intuition.

Making And Using Moon Water

You have already been introduced to the concept of Moon water—when you are purifying and charging your objects, you are utilizing Moon water. All you have to do to create Moon water is left purified water out overnight, allowing it to bathe in Full Moon's light. The next morning, your Moon water is ready. Make sure that you save it for use during times that there is no Full Moon readily available—place it into a bottle with a label on it. Of course, you can always try using the colors of your container to create the intention that you wish to imbue to your water, or you can choose to add a crystal to your water as you create it. Of course, however, you should always check to ensure that any crystal you use is safe in water.

When you make Moon water, it can vary slightly from month to month. This is because the Moon water that you are creating will take on certain characteristics or properties of whichever sign correlates with that particular Moon. This means that sometimes, you will see entirely different results altogether form what you may have expected. Here is a list of the properties that your water will absorb depending on the Moon it was exposed to:

- **Moon in Aries:** This energy is positive and can help imbue you with courage and the fortitude necessary to face anything. This particular Moon water is the perfect choice if you need to charge a magical weapon.

- **Moon in Taurus:** This energy is stable and fertile. It is strong and constant, like the Earth.

- **Moon in Gemini:** This energy is positive—it is associated with defeating and overcoming any challenges that may get in your way.

- **Moon in Cancer:** This energy is loving and protective—it is associated with maternal feelings.

- **Moon in Leo:** This energy is creative and lucky—it is the perfect energy to use when going into politics or something else that will put you in the public eye.

- **Moon in Virgo:** This energy is largely practical—it will aid in the attention necessary to really fully plan out actions and details.

- **Moon in Libra:** This energy is balanced. It is persuasive, loving, and is useful in attempting to get to the bottom of conflict or other legal sorts of issues.

- **Moon in Scorpio:** This energy is spiritual and psychic—it is often used to banish or cleanse.

- **Moon in Sagittarius:** This energy is transforming—it aids with meditation and self-reflection.

- **Moon in Capricorn:** This energy is related to success in careers and wealth.

- **Moon in Aquarius:** This energy is considered creative, innovative, and facilitative of invention.

- **Moon in Pisces:** This energy is associated with dreams—it is perfect for attempting to engage in astral projection.

With your Moon water created, it is time to ensure it is properly stored—many people prefer to keep their Moon water in darkness any time it is not using, hoping to avoid infecting it with foreign energy that may penetrate it otherwise. Your bottle choice is important to keep in mind, ensuring that it is chosen appropriately. Specific colors are usually associated with specific intentions, such as:

- **Colorless:** This is perfect if you wish for clarity, healing, and focus.
- **Frosted white:** This is perfect to embody the energy from the Moon herself, as well as the protection and healing of others.
- **Pink:** A development of self-love, protection, and even healing.
- **Red:** This is perfect for reflecting passion and romance.
- **Amber:** This is associated with animals and protection
- **Green:** This is associated with wealth and health.
- **Blue:** This is associated with healing, divination, and peace
- **Purple:** This is associated with magic, protection, and power.

When you are mixing your Moon water, there is one more thing to remember—certain items are not appropriate to mix into the water at all. These items may become damaged when exposed to the water, or they can cause other issues with the items or stones that were placed within it. Just because most stones are not reactive in water, does not mean that all stones are not reactive, and that property must be kept in mind. There is actually a list of stones that should be kept out of the water entirely. These stones may fall apart, rust, crack, or otherwise fall apart, as a direct result of being dropped into water, such as:

- Calcite
- Mica
- Turquoise
- Selenite
- Labradorite
- Carnelian
- Galena
- Obsidian

- Pearls

- Malachite

- Lodestone

- Moldavite

- Opals

Instead, you can keep these stones near or on top of the container holding the water. In doing so, you still allow the body to absorb the magic of the Moon.

Chapter 4: Making Sense Of Lunar Rhythms And Dynamics

Now, we are going to return back to a bit more of the basic information about the Moon and its rhythms that you will need to understand. In first understanding the rhythm of the Moon, you can start to understand Sabbats and the Lunar Cycle itself. The Moon's orbit around the Earth, its journey from point A to B is relatively straightforward—it happens day in and day out, with the Moon constantly circling the Earth as the Earth circles the Sun.

Sabbats And Seasons

The seasons come and go just as reliably as the cycle of the Moon—they change the world around you and impact how life lives. The seasons change how the plants grow, influence wildlife to breed and reproduce, and even can control migration patterns of several species, depending on which season it is. Plants do not always grow year-round, and several either die or go into hibernation during the winter months.

The passing of the seasons is celebrated within Wiccan holidays, particularly in the Wheel of the Year. Four of the Sabbats, in particular, marked the changing of the seasons from one to the next. These were considered the Lesser Sabbats, if you remember correctly—these were the equinoxes and solstices that are used to mark the change of the seasons. The two equinoxes mark the change from winter to spring and from summer to autumn. During these days, the length of daytime and nighttime is equal. The solstices, then, mark the change from autumn to winter and from spring to summer. During the summer solstice, the day is the longest it will be during that year. During the winter solstice, conversely, the night is the longest that it will be during the year.

These solstices and equinoxes became proper Sabbats, with Wiccans recognizing the power and the need to honor those important moments in which the world is full of energy that is spurring the change in cycles. Remember, the changing of the seasons can be directly related to the life cycle of the Triple Goddess, noting how spring and the Maiden can be related, while summer is reminiscent to the Mother, with autumn associated with the Crone, and finally, death in the winter.

The Greater Sabbats, then, are somewhere between the changes of the seasons, honoring each of the seasons and marking that change is coming soon. These Sabbats, Imbolc, Beltaine, Lughnasadh, and Samhain are important to celebrate as well, recognizing the importance of each and every holiday.

When you use the magic of the Sabbats, you will find that the power that is being released around you has increased, and you can tap into it as a result.

You can celebrate the passing of the seasons, celebrating the Sabbats and tapping into their vast powers.

Following The Lunar Cycle

The Lunar Cycle, the 28 days during which the Moon transforms from a New Moon to the Full Moon and back again, is incredibly powerful. This ebb and flow of power, similar to the rise and fall of the tides directly influences your body and the world around you. This is undeniable. When you learn to understand the Lunar Cycle, you can start to identify which times during the cycle you should use for any particular event or planning in intentions. If you know when to set your goals, act on intentions, and let go, you can start to figure out how to best utilize the energy from the Moon.

New Moon

During this stage, the Moon is not visible at night, and this marks the beginning of the Lunar Cycle itself, starting off the 3-day period of darkness. As a beginning, this time is pregnant with potential—anything could come next because nothing has started at this point, meaning that it is developing and can become anything. This time is the best time to figure out what your intentions will be for this Lunar Cycle, and this time is associated with the Fool Major Arcana in Tarot.

Crescent Moon

Shortly after the New Moon begins the Crescent Moon. This is day 3-7 within the 28-day cycle. During this period of time, energy is beginning to build up, though it has not yet really developed into much. The more the Moon begins to widen and swell, the more energy is emanated outward. While you may not be inherently aware of this energy at first, before you have had the chance to develop an affinity for sensing energies, it is there waiting for you. Still, focus on your intentions for that particular cycle and prepare for the month and utilizing the energy that is yet to come.

First Quarter Moon

During days 7 through 10 of the cycle, you will find yourself in the First Quarter Moon. During this period, you can now see a solid half-circle in the sky above you when you look up at night. At this point, 25% of the way through the cycle, you should have a solid idea of what your intentions are, and it is time to begin acting upon them. Just as the Moon expands and grows, so too should your resolve and determination to act according to your intentions. During this period, you should create a plan to achieve your intentions, no matter what they are.

Gibbous Moon

At this stage, the Moon has almost filled. This is day 10-15 of the Lunar Cycle, and during this time, the Moon will grow daily, slowly expanding and swelling, much like the Mother she is representing at this stage. At this point in the cycle, you want to act. Remember, the Full Moon is one of the peaks in energy, and you are almost there! Make sure that you are continuing to strive toward those intentions that you have set without fail—no matter how tempting quitting may be at this point, persevere and keep moving forward. You are almost there.

Full Moon

This is the peak of energy within the Lunar Calendar. It will peak between the 15th and 18th day of that particular cycle. This is the moment of truth—when you find out how successful you were when it comes to summoning your intentions and making them a reality. You should be able to tell now whether you will actually achieve those intentions or if you will have to try again in the future. At this stage, push past any final reservations that stand between you and your intentions and make them happen. If you cannot for some reason, then let it go and rest. Honor the Full Moon and release any negativity that may have prevented your success in the first place.

Disseminating Moon

At this point, the Moon is waning—it is shrinking with each and every passing day. You will see this during the 18th-21st days of the Lunar Cycle, and as you see this period pass, remember that this time is about accepting the end results of your process and letting go if you do not like what has happened. This period of time is perfect for resting as the Moon's energy is lessening on a daily basis. Breathe and allow yourself a period to rest instead of dwelling further on the matters.

Last Quarter Moon

Now, the moon is continuing to shrink—it has reached the stage of a semicircle once more somewhere between days 21 and 24, marking the ending of your journey. Remember to continue to rest during these days. You can meditate to start to think about what has happened, self-reflecting and reflecting upon what the universe's energy is telling you. You can also try to identify how you think the next cycle will go as well, or you can even start to plan out your next cycle altogether. One thing is for sure at this stage, however—you should absolutely focus on some serious introspection as you prepare for the New Moon.

Balsamic Moon

At this stage, the moon is little more than a tiny crescent within the sky. It is just barely visible compared to a New Moon, and at this point, after day 25, you find that your cycle is wrapping to a close. Again, allow yourself to rest and prepare for the soon-to-be-present New Moon once more. Just exist in the moment, really absorbing the world around you and celebrate anything that has gone well in your life thus far. Remember to thank the universe and begin to identify what you would like the next long-term plan to be.

Special Phases of the Moon

Beyond the eight primary points in time with the Moon, there are several special phases of the Moon as well, most notably, the Blue Moon, the Lunar Eclipse, and the Black Moon. While these special phases do not happen often, they are still important as you go through the process of developing your own connection to Wicca and the Moon in the first place.

- **The Blue Moon:** This is what happens when two Full Moons pass within the same month period. The second Full Moon gets referred to as a Blue Moon. The powers of the Moon during a Blue Moon are more powerful than that of a typical Full Moon, and if you have the pleasure of experiencing one of these, you should absolutely make it a point to tap into that energy. However, approach with caution—the Blue Moon's energy can vary greatly, and the end result after you have cast your intention may be vastly different from what you had intended.

- **The Lunar Eclipse:** Eclipses are powerful events. During an Eclipse, you will be able to feel the shift, the change from one event or pattern into another. This energy can be tapped into in order to make decisions that you may otherwise struggle with. This is perfect for seeking out intuition, tapping into the messages that the universe is whispering to you.

- **The Black Moon:** Unlike the Eclipse and Blue Moon, both of which happen sporadically, the Black Moon is a part of each and every Lunar Cycle. The Black Moon is the last night of the Lunar Cycle, right before the birth of the New Moon. During this time, it is time to focus on the darkness within you—everyone has this, so do not be ashamed. This is the time to start analyzing your nightmares, facing your fears, and otherwise engaging in magic related to the shadows.

Chapter 5: The Lunar Cycle And Its Correspondences To Magick

With that established idea of the Lunar Cycle and how it fluctuates throughout the month, as well as how the Moon's change in phases can influence how much energy is being released, it is time to start looking at the correspondences between each phase of the Lunar Cycle and the Magick associated with each. As you do this, you then start to develop a better understanding of exactly which forms of magic you can use when for the best impact and result. Of course, then in Chapter 8, after learning about intentions and rituals, you will be provided with several spells that can be used, particularly when influenced and bolstered by the Moon's several phases.

The Dark Moon

As already established, the Dark Moon is the time of the month in which the Moon is entirely shrouded in darkness. It represents the Goddess in the form of the Crone, honoring the Goddess Hecate, and is a point in the Lunar Cycle at which the negative energies that have accumulated should be released and banished. During the Dark Moon Esbats, it is important to stop and recognize the differences between each other, and the mysteries that enshroud this period time. During this period of time, it is a good time to practice scrying to develop more intuition.

The Dark Moon goes by several names—in fact, the name of the Dark Moon changes from month to month. You can tell exactly which Dark Moon is being discussed if you pay attention to the names used to refer to it.

- **The Dark Quiet Moon:** January
- **The Dark Hunger Moon:** February
- **The Dark Seed Moon:** March
- **The Dark Planting Moon:** April
- **The Dark Ninth Moon:** May
- **The Dark Strawberry Moon:** June
- **The Dark Blessing Moon:** July
- **The Dark Harvest Moon:** August
- **The Dark Singing Moon:** September
- **The Dark Falling Leaf Moon:** October
- **The Dark Dead Moon:** November
- **The Dark Snow Moon:** December

Each of these names, if you look at them, seems to symbolize something more than themselves—named for some specific reason that closely related to what was happening in the world around them. The Snow Moon, for example, happens in December, the beginning of winter for most people. The Strawberry Moon is associated with the time during which strawberries ripen and so on.

The New Moon

The New Moon is a time during which beginnings are celebrated. The magick that is most likely to stick during these times are those involving cycles and beginnings, such as new habits, new diets, or new studies. As the Goddess is in her Infant form, curious and interested in the world around her, so too will you enter the world with this energy, tapping into it to encourage the changes you wish to see. Just as the Goddess has become a young infant, bound by curiosity, and requiring development to really move forward, you, too, will draw from that. You will be able to trigger that very same development in yourself.

The Waxing Moon

The Waxing Moon involves a recognition of the Goddess entering her Maiden form. She has grown and developed from an infant into a young woman, just before she is capable of developing and giving birth. During this stage, she continues to grow and mature. She is not yet where she needs to be or where she could be, and that is okay—this is a cyclical process. Take this opportunity to bathe in the growth of energy that comes from her developing and growing herself. During this period of time, particularly in the days just prior to the growth into the Full Moon, you are best served with magick that will provide you with something. This could be a job or a home, it could be good luck, or it could be the discovery of someone new, or even the conception of a child.

During this stage, you are recognizing the journey of the Maiden, who is seeking to identify and discover a partner with whom she can become a mother. She is energetic, and that energy, though powerful, can almost seem restless at times. Use this magic and the swelling of the energy levels to help yourself.

The First Quarter Moon

The Moon is continuing to swell and grow, and at its peak here, it has reached about 75% illumination. The Moon is still growing and developing, picking up energy. She usually rises during the afternoon hours, getting closer to midnight on a daily basis. She is excited and energetic, and we are bathed in her enthusiasm. Nevertheless, despite this enthusiasm, we are still not at our greatest potential. Nevertheless, move forward—use the momentum and the growth of the Moon and the Goddess to push yourself forward as well. You can keep moving toward the goals and intentions you have set.

During this stage, you are best served through utilizing the energy of the Moon and channeling it into planning and organization. You can use the Moon's growing energy and motivation to push yourself into productivity—just as the Goddess pushes toward having her child, you push toward personal growth as well. You can use this for the growth of your self-esteem, or you can use it to better yourself in other ways, choosing to go through with exercise, changes to your routine or otherwise attempting to change yourself. This period of time is also fantastic for influencing your intention for pregnancy if you wish to have a child.

The Waxing Gibbous Moon

The Waxing Gibbous Moon continues to swell outward, giving it an appearance reminiscent of a pregnant woman. It is round on one end while the other is swelling out. During this stage, your intentions are grown and developed until their birth at the Full Moon. This moon, in particular, rises in the afternoon before setting around 3 in the morning each day.

During this phase of the Moon, you want to continue growth spells. As the Moon continues to grow and swell, you can tap into that same energy, allowing your own personal growth to continue. If you are low in self-esteem, you can tap into the

Moon's magic, allowing yourself to draw on her own confidence and growth to bolster your own confidence instead. During this period, as well, you want to begin preparing for the Full Moon as it quickly approaches. You want to make sure you wrap up any last-minute preparations for your Full Moon magic.

The Waning Moon

Now, just for a moment, we are going to skip over the Full Moon and to the Waning Moon's magick— this is intentional. The Full Moon's magick has several aspects that will be considered, so let's first touch upon the Waning Moon and the Goddess's Crone phase before continuing.

These days are the days just before the Dark Moon. During this period, the Moon's energy is starting to drain down, and just as the magick begins to ebb, you can push with it the negative energy as well. This is the perfect time to let the energies of the universe take away the negativity from your life to clear the way for the rebirth of the Goddess. As her light fades away, so too does her strength, but despite that loss of strength comes a great advantage—she has gained wisdom during her period of growth. Even though her light will completely disappear, the cycle of rebirth will begin again.

During this period of time, you want to engage in personal reflection. You can stop, reflect upon what has happened throughout this last Lunar Cycle and prepare for what you are looking forward to during the next cycle. Learn from her wisdom, learn to reflect, and learn to really analyze yourself as you rest.

The Full Moon

Now, back to the Full Moon. During this period of time, when the Moon is full, you will recognize the Goddess for what she is—a Mother. At this point, all of the intentions, magick, and energy you have been projecting outwards have fully gestated and are ready to be born. During this phase, then, magick and energy levels are at their highest. At this stage, you can redirect the energy and magick from the Moon, absorbing it into water, purifying items, or even consecrating any tools that you will be using throughout the month.

During this phase, the Moon is the Mother figure—she loves and cares for her children, all of the Earth, and this time is often celebrated with the Esbat. These Full Moons have very specific names for each, as well as corresponding spirits, herbs, flowers, scents, trees, animals, birds, and Gods and Goddesses. As you can see, there is plenty that goes into each of these Full Moons that make them powerful and compelling, and this is exactly why this section was pushed past the Waning moon, despite the shift backward in time.

December Full Moon

While the calendar year may start with January, the Wheel of the Year begins with December. The Full

Moon of December is known as the *Ice Moon*, though there are several other names that it could also be referred to as. Sometimes, you will hear this moon referred to as the Big Winter Moon, the Wolf Moon, the Moon of the Long Nights, or the Oak Moon.

During this month, you should spend time planning your goals for the coming year. This is the beginning of the year and at this point, it is time to start acting accordingly. As the Earth freezes (at least in the Northern Hemisphere), it is time to honor the cycle of death and rebirth. The plants have died—the trees have shed their leaves, but you know that spring and rebirth is just around the corner, and you learn to recognize this and respect it. During this period, you will be best served through meditation and contemplation—spend time remembering those that you have lost, and how you can strengthen your own spiritual self.

There are several affinities associated with this Moon in particular, including:

- **Spirits:** Faeries (Snow, Storm, and Winter Tree Faeries)
- **Herbs:** Mistletoe, holly, English ivy, and fir
- **Flowers:** Poinsettias Christmas cactuses, and Holly
- **Scents:** Violet, Frankincense, Lilac, Patchouli, and Rose Geranium
- **Trees:** Holly tree, the pine tree, and the fir tree
- **Animals and birds:** The rook, the deer, the snowy owl, the mouse, the bear, the robin, and the horse
- **Gods:** Hecate, Osiris, Minerva, Hathor, Athene, Ixchel, and Norns

January Full Moon

The Full Moon of January is known as the *Wolf Moon*. This is still the beginning of the Wheel of the Year, and as such, it is also a fantastic time to focus on beginning and planning. While it is difficult to find motivation, especially with those shorter days and cold weather, this is the perfect time to work on personal growth and reflection. The more you reflect inward, the less outward energy you have to expend, and you likely have some problems of your own to reconcile with. During this time, spells for protection and reversal is best.

- **Spirits:** Brownies and gnomes.
- **Herbs:** Holy thistle, various different cones or nuts, and marjoram
- **Flowers:** Crocus and snowdrop flowers
- **Scents:** The Mimosa tree and Musk
- **Trees:** The Birch tree.
- **Animals and birds:** Fox, coyote, bluejay, and pheasant.
- **Gods:** Sinn, Freya, Saraswati, Inanna, and Ch'ang-O

February Full Moon

During February, the Earth is still frozen—this Full Moon is known as the *Ice Moon* thanks to the prevalence of ice during this time. Spring is just around the corner but has not yet arrived yet, so take this time to finish readying yourself for the major growth and development of Spring and Summer. During this period, you should focus on spells that will help you purify yourself and your home. During this period, you should develop an ability to accept what has happened in the past and move on to the future. Forgive yourself from anything that has gone wrong, learning from the great, wise Crone as she prepares to be reborn once more, and focus on loving and healing yourself.

- **Spirits:** House Faeries
- **Herbs:** Sage, myrrh, the balm of Gilead, spikenard, and hyssop
- **Flowers:** Heliotrope and Wisteria
- **Scents:** Mimosa and Musk
- **Trees:** Cedar, rowan, and laurel trees

- **Animals and birds:** This Moon put a heavy emphasis on the unicorn, the eagle, the otter, and the chickadee.
- **Gods:** Aphrodite, Persephone, Diana, Juno, Demeter, Kuan Yin, and Brigid

March Full Moon

With the arrival of March and the Vernal Equinox, so too comes the arrival of spring and the *Storm Moon*. Known due to the constant storms that are associated with springtime rains that bring life back to the Earth, this month is associated with luck, freedom, and prosperity. Thanks to the Equinox bringing a balance between the day and night, and the light and dark, you will have extra luck if you work with spells that are meant to help you shatter illusions and reveal the truth.

- **Spirits:** Merpeople
- **Herbs:** Irish moss, broom, yellow dock, wood betony, and High John Root

- **Flowers:** The flowers relevant to this period include violets, daffodils, and jonquil

- **Scents:** With the arrival of spring comes the arrival of floral scents, such as apple blossoms and honeysuckle

- **Trees:** Dogwood and Alder

- **Animals and Birds:** Boar, hedgehog, cougar, sea eagle, and sea crow

- **Gods:** Luna, Artemis, Athene, Minerva, Astarte, Cybele, Hecate, Isis, the Morrigan

April Full Moon

As spring is in full bloom, April's Moon earns the name of *Growing Moon*. This moon is all about production, creation, and restoration of balance. During this time, focus on magick meant for self-confidence, self-reliance, and to grow and change. In particular, this is the perfect month for meditation or prayer that will help with anger management or to regulate selfishness.

- **Spirits:** Plant faeries

- **Herbs:** Dragons blood, thistle, geranium, chives, and herbs
- **Flowers:** Sweet peas and daisy
- **Scents:** Patchouli, bergamot, bay, and pine
- **Trees:** The hazel, pine, and bay trees
- **Animals and birds:** Wolf, bear, magpie, and hawk
- **Gods:** Bast, Venus, Ishtar, Ceres, Hathor, Anahita, and Kali

May Full Moon

Do you remember the chart with regions for planting? Most of those plants were intended to be planted within the month of May, bringing us to May's *Planting Moon*. This Full Moon is a time in which creative and reproduction energy flows readily. During this time, there is stronger contact with the spiritual realm than in other Moons. At this time, try to bond better to any of your spiritual guides, aides, or guardians.

- **Spirits:** Faeries and elves.

- **Herbs:** Yarrow, thyme, rose, mugwort, mint, Dittany of Crete
- **Flowers:** Broom, rose, lily of the valley, foxglove
- **Scents:** Sandalwood and rose
- **Trees:** The Hawthorn tree
- **Animals and Birds:** Swan, leopard, dove, lynx, swallow, cat
- **Gods:** The Horned God, Pan, Artemis, Maia, Diana, Aphrodite, Venus, and Bast

June Full Moon

June's Full Moon is a time of rest known as the *Mead Moon*—the planting has been done and now what is left is growth. During this time, you will find the most luck utilizing spells and rituals for protection, strength, and preventing future issues. During this time, you should make sure to involve plenty of self-reflection, making sure you make decisions that are appropriate for you and your life. During this time, you reach the time in which the light outweighs the darkness with the arrival of summer.

- **Spirits:** Sylphs and Zephyrs
- **Herbs:** Moss, parsley, tansy, vervain, dog grass, skullcap, and meadowsweet
- **Flowers:** Yarrow, orchid, and lavender
- **Scents:** Lavender and lily of the valley
- **Trees:** The Oaktree
- **Animals and birds:** Peacock, toad, wren, frog, monkey, and butterfly
- **Gods:** Ishtar, Cerridwen, Neith, Green Man, Bendis, Isis, and Aine of Knockaine

July Full Moon

In July, summer is in full swing. During this time, energy is relaxed as growth continues, leading up to autumn and the harvest. Now is your last chance to take advantage of waiting for the harvest, and you can look at the bounty of your crops that you have sown, preparing to benefit from them. During this time, focus on meditation and divination for your goals and plans.

- **Spirits:** Crop Faeries and hobgoblins
- **Herbs:** Hyssop, lemon balm, agrimony, and honeysuckle
- **Flowers:** Jasmine, water lily, and lotus
- **Scents:** Frankincense
- **Trees:** Ash, acacia, and oak
- **Animals and birds:** Swallow, whale, ibis, dolphin, turtle, starling, and crab
- **Gods:** Venus, Nephtys, Cerridwen, Holda, Hel, Juno, Athena, and Khepera

August Full Moon

August brings with it the harvest, and appropriately, it is known as the *Corn Moon*. At this time, there is a celebration of health and vitality, as well as a celebration of the friendships that had to come together to make the harvest happen. During this time, focus on dreamwork and meditation about the harvest, making sure that you send your own thanks back into the Universe as you welcome the harvest that you have grown.

- **Spirits:** Dryads
- **Herbs:** Rue, fennel, bay, angelica, St. John's wort, and chamomile
- **Flowers:** Marigold and sunflowers
- **Scents:** Heliotrope and frankincense
- **Trees:** Cedar, alder, and hazel
- **Animals and birds:** Eagle, dragon, sphinx, phoenix, falcon, crane, and lion
- **Gods:** Nemesis, Hecate, Diana, Thoth, Hathor, Ganesha

September Full Moon

In September, you are once again approaching another Equinox, and as such, it brings another balance of light and dark. You have sown and reaped your harvest, earning this Moon the name of *Harvest Moon,* and as you approach winter, it is time to rest. Your time as a nurturer, much like how the Goddess reaches the Mother phase, is coming to an end, and it is now time to reflect on the wisdom of your harvest and year. Take this time to reflect on the past, organize your home, as well as your mind and soul, and prepare for winter.

- **Spirits:** Trooping faeries
- **Herbs:** Skullcap, valerian, wheat, rye, fennel, copal
- **Flowers:** Lily and narcissus
- **Scents:** Bergamot, gardenia, mastic, and storax
- **Trees:** The bay, larch, and hazel trees
- **Animals and birds:** Jackal, ibis, snake, and sparrow
- **Gods:** Thoth, Ch'ang-O, Nephtys, Ceres, Isis, Demeter

October Full Moon

With this Moon marks the arrival of the *Blood Moon,* named for the older processes of slaughtering livestock right around this month, before winter weather can make an appearance. During this Moon, you will prepare for Samhain, recognizing the change that is about to arrive. During this time, energy shifts to entice you to pull inwards rather than expanding external energy. Use this month to prepare for the long winter that is ahead. During this Moon, magic that is just and seeking balance, as well as cleansing and harmony, are particularly potent.

- **Spirits:** Frost and plant faeries
- **Herbs:** Burdock, angelica, catnip, thyme, pennyroyal
- **Flowers:** Cosmos, marigold, and calendula
- **Scents:** Cherry, apple blossom, and strawberry
- **Trees:** Yew and cypress
- **Animals and birds:** Robin, scorpion, ram, crow, elephant, jackal, heron, and stag
- **Gods:** Hathor, Belili, the Horned God, Lakshmi, Kore, Demeter, Astarte, and Ishtar

November Full Moon

The November Moon brings with it again the arrival of freezing temperatures and the shift into winter. The Full Moon during this season is known as the *Snow Moon.* During this time, you are grounding yourself as you prepare to last through the winter, allowing yourself to reflect and transform. Spend this time connecting with the spirits and Gods and Goddesses that you relate to.

- **Spirits:** Underground Faeries
- **Herbs:** Blessed thistle, cinquefoil, betony, verbena, borage, and grains of paradise
- **Flowers:** Chrysanthemum and blooming cacti
- **Scents:** Lemon, peppermint, cedar, narcissus, hyacinth, and cherry blossom
- **Trees:** Cypress and alder
- **Animals and birds:** Sparrow, jackal, crocodile, goose, scorpion, unicorn, and owl
- **Gods:** Sarasvati, Osiris, Skadi, Bast, Lakshmi, Hecate, Nicnevin, Kali, Isis

Chapter 6: Powerful Methods To Achieve Your Goals Using Lunar Magick

The possibilities are as endless as the sky above you when it comes to utilizing Lunar Magick for your own good. When you decide that you wish to really achieve your goals, there are several different ways for you to channel, direct, and regulate the energies of both yourself and the universe and Moon, allowing you to make major changes in the world around you.

New Moon Magick And Rituals

The New Moon's magick is free for you to influence. It is readily flowing into the world around you, and if you learn how best to tap into it, you can start to direct it accordingly with your own intentions and energy. This section will guide you through several of your options for interacting with New Moon energy and magick.

Intention and Attraction

In particular, during the New Moon, there is potential that is untapped, undirected, and entirely available to be redirected and guided. This means that you can tap into the lunar cycle's magick, recognizing that the energy is currently pure, and because of that, when you set an intention for the energy, you can start to regulate and alter it. One such way of doing so is through the Law of Attraction.

Law of Attraction

The Law of Attraction is as simple as if you wish for it, you can attract it. When you wish, you send out an interest into the universe, and that then draws your interest closer to you. However, you need to do more than simply wish for it—there are steps you can take to maximize your attraction.

1. Write your wish or intention onto a piece of paper in one sentence.

2. Make sure your sentence uses positive verbs and stays within the present tense.

3. Pretend that your wish is already true and happening as you sit there.

4. Visualize how you feel, utilizing all of your senses to fully and truly create the idea that you are attracting the intention.

5. Meditate on how you felt, as well as how you would like it.

6. Now, let go of any expectations that you have around you. In putting trust in the Universe that what will happen will be brought to you.

New Moon Witchcraft

Now, instead of just sending out intentions for the Universe to provide for you, you can use other methods instead. There are magickal methods that you can use—you can prefer spells or rituals as well, including, but not limited to:

- **Attraction**
- **Binding**
- **Blessing**

- **Consecration**
- **Divination**
- **Summoning**

Each of these methods will be discussed at the end of this book in a guide for you with step-by-step tutorials to walk you through the process. As you learn these steps, you will find yourself developing more and more of a magickal repertoire that you can use, allowing you to truly tap into the Earth's energy and that of the Moon and the Goddess as well.

Full Moon Magick And Rituals

As already discussed, the Full Moon sees the most energy that is available to you. While the New Moon's energy is largely impressionable and shaped, you use the Full Moon's magick then to purify and protect. Of course, this involves several processes, and there are many, many different options that you can use through this process. Think of this chapter as a brief glimpse into what is possible, and you will then see more as you get to the end of this book.

Giving Thanks to the Full Moon

When the time comes, you must give thanks to the Full Moon for all of the wonderful energy it provides for you. The best way to do this is to let go of your expectations. This is when you find out if the intentions you set during the full moon came to fruition—if they did not, you need to reflect and identify why. If they did, you still should celebrate the success. Either way, it is time to forgive yourself, look forward, and provide thanks to the Full Moon. Let go of your old intentions to make space for the new. You can do this through what is known as a release ritual.

Release Ritual

Release rituals are important to allow yourself to really let go of the old intentions, making space for the new and allowing for the growth you need for the future. In releasing old intentions back into the universe, they may make their way back to you, or they will disappear, but either way, you are in no worse of a position than you are at that particular moment.

When you are ready, releasing your intentions and the past is quite simple. There are several options for you, but one, in particular, involves making a list—under the Full Moon's light, write down the bad that has happened during the month. Markdown anything significant as you do so. Name each and every person involved, and then forgive them all. As you have forgiven them, speaking the words out loud, burn the paper and release the ashes. With the ashes, let your ill will fly into the wind as well.

If you are releasing your New Moon intentions, try reading out everything that you had planned for the month. After glancing over them, tell yourself, out loud, that you have chosen to release the intentions into the universe. For example, "I am relinquishing my intentions to the Universe. May it be for the best." After speaking the words, burn the paper that has your list of intentions.

Other Spells for the Full Moon

Beyond intentions and releasing, there are several other spell options that you can use. Again, just as with the New Moon magick, the spells that are listed here will be discussed in detail in Chapter 8.

- **Banishment**
- **Purification**
- **Healing**
- **Charging and activating spells**
- **Protection spells**
- **Cleansing and Charging tools**
- **Making Moon Water**
- **Drawing Down the Moon**

Honor Your Blessings

After you have let go, however, there is one last thing you must do—you need to honor your blessings. When you do this, you are essentially performing a gratitude ritual, and in doing so, you are releasing negativity in order to replace it with positive feelings and intentions. Every time you release something, be it positivity or negativity, something else must fill that gap, so by releasing the negative and creating positive feelings of gratitude, you can fill the gap yourself. This can be done in several different ways—choose one that works best for you:

- Pour a glass of wine or another drink of your choice. With every sip you take, speak the words of something that you can give thanks for or that you are grateful for. At the last drop of wine, allow it to spill to the ground.

- Write down several things that you are grateful for onto a piece of paper and allow yourself to fill with gratefulness. Speak out loud what was on your list, and then burn the list, allowing yourself to reflect on the gratefulness.

- Try self-blessing: Right after a bath, step out without a towel and allow yourself to air dry. In the mirror, tell yourself that you are a good person. Make sure that you reiterate it to yourself, convincing yourself that what you say is true— "I truly love this person— S/he is one of the children of the God and Goddess, and they love him/her." With oil, anoint your body part—start at your feet and bless each and every part. Thank the God and Goddess for your feet, your knees, your genitalia, your heart, your lips, your eyes, and yourself. In doing so, saying, "Blessed be my [body part here], so I can [insert action here]," you are giving thanks for each part of you.

At the end of the spell, you can look in the mirror and say that you are blessed and that you will grow and flourish. With the spell over, release the energy that you have built up into the ground. Spend some time gazing up at the Full Moon after, offering thanks to the God and Goddess for aiding you in the process, and then make sure you record down your thoughts on the process.

Chapter 7: Preparation And Rituals For Spellcasting

You may be feeling anxious, interested in arriving in the spellcasting portion of this book, and I cannot fault you for that! There is something truly exhilarating about being able to cast a spell of your own volition, feeling the energy as it flows within you. As tempting as it may be to skip ahead, make it a point to read through this chapter—it will provide you with all of the background information you will need, teaching you the ins and outs of spellcasting, preparation, and the most basic rituals that you will use.

Spellcasting 101

Spellcasting itself is so important—it is integral to Wicca and magic in general. When you are spellcasting, you are sending out your intentions— you are making it a point to make it clear to your spell and to the universe what you wish to have come back to you. If you are doing a spell, you can then redirect your own energy, and as this happens, you will feel like you are really changing the world around you, simply by influencing your own energy to influence the energy of everything around you.

Self-Dedication

Perhaps one of the first rituals you will learn as you begin the path of Wicca is the Self-Dedication ritual. This is you dedicating yourself to the God and Goddess—it is allowing you to build and solidify that relationship with the great Deities, and it shows that you are dedicated to serving the Deities as well. When you do this, declaring your spirituality, you want to make sure that you really mean it when you do—this should not be taken lightly and you should be positive that it is what you legitimately wish to do.

Before beginning to go through the steps, first, let's look at a handful of important tips before beginning. These tips, if you keep them in mind, can help the process go smoother.

- This can be done at any point during the Lunar Cycle, aside from the New Moon.
- Make sure you will not be bothered or interrupted at all—either do this entirely alone at home or behind locked doors.
- Make sure you are alone and serious in the commitment

Preparation

Some people choose to go through all of the fanfare to make it formal and ritualized—they may choose to go through a ritualized bath, or perhaps they use tools that they have meticulously crafted on their own, and others can choose a name that they feel encompasses their spiritual side, allowing you to greet the Deities and use your new, spiritual, magickal name. Ultimately, this is an incredibly personal endeavor and you should choose to do so however works best for you.

Go over this ritual beforehand, and if you feel like you may not recall it all at first, try entering it into a Book of Shadows—this is a book in which you record all important information, such as the laws of your coven, observations, and thoughts. Beyond that, it should include a dedication, the Gods and Goddesses that you have chosen to follow, correspondence tables that will help you keep track of everything, spells, divinations, and more. Essentially, anything related to your practice should be recorded within your Book of Shadows.

The Essentials

When you are dedicating yourself, you will need three simple items at your altar: Blessing oil, salt to purify the ground, and a white candle. With those three simple tools, and your Book of Shadows or any altar tools that you may choose to incorporate, you are ready to begin. Please remember that this is a template—you should be free to change this in any way necessary to ensure that the process is exactly as you want it.

This ritual, ideally, is done skyclad—this means naked, if you are not well-versed in the terms that you will be learning during your journey into Wicca. In a quiet, preferably private area, prepare yourself. Make sure any distractions are turned off and stowed away.

The Ritual

Now, ground yourself, using deep breathing and mindfulness methods. This can be done through meditation or any other form that you prefer—make sure that you shut out the world around you and instead retreat internally to your own heart and mind, focusing instead entirely on your own feeling of peace.

Take the salt and pour some onto the floor—just a sprinkle will do. It will help purify the ground. Step onto the salt and light the candle. As you do so, place your hand near the flame, allowing yourself to absorb the warmth and enjoy the pleasant sensation. As you gaze into the flickering flame, stop, and really think about what you hope to gain out of this journey. What is motivating you right at that moment? What is driving you to dedicate yourself to new Deities right at that moment?

With those thoughts in mind, stand in front of the altar and the candle. Speak the following words (or something similar):

I declare that I am a child of the God and Goddess—I ask them in this moment to bless me as a child of Them.

At this point, touch the blessing oil and anoint, or rub, it onto your forehead. Some people may choose to draw a spiritual shape that really resonates with them, such as a pentagram, while others may simply smudge it onto their skin. Choose whatever works best for you and feels right. Now, continue speaking out loud:

Please bless my mind, granting me the ability to accept the great God and Goddess's wisdom.

Now, anoint your eyelids, very carefully to not get it into your eyes and continue:

Please bless my eyes, granting me the clarity to see the path set out before me.

It is time to anoint the nose—just the tip.

Please bless my nose, allowing me to breathe the divine essence of the great Deities.

Move down to your lips.

Please bless my lips, granting the fortitude to choose to speak respectfully, truthfully, and honorably.

Now, the chest:

Please bless my heart, so I may be free to be loved, as well as love others as I love myself.

Anoint the tops of your hands:

Please bless my hands, granting me the strength necessary to help and heal those around me who may be in need.

Now, move to the genitals:

May my [womb/penis] receive your blessing to aid in the creation of life.

Move down to your feet and anoint the soles:

Please bless my feet, providing me the support I need to walk along the path of the great Divine Ones.

At this point, declare any loyalty to whichever deities you have chosen to honor and follow. This is just as personal as the rest of this process. If you are unsure if you will follow any in particular, you can always use "God and Goddess," or even "Mother and Father" to continue this process.

I pledge my loyalty and dedication to [god name here]. I vow to walk alongside them, following their guidance on this great spiritual journey. I vow to honor them and request that they grant me permission to become closer to them. As I will it, so it shall be.

Now, spend some time meditating before ending this process. Bathe in the energy that you have absorbed and see if you feel any closer to the Deities. After this process, if you are free to do so, try to sleep.

Casting A Circle

As you read through several of the spells in the next chapter, you will notice that several will ask that you cast a circle—but if you are new to this process, you may not even know what this is in the first place. It is essentially the energy that you are building up around you—you effectively will imagine that you are surrounded by a circle of energy, willing the energy of the Universe to flow around you and create the circle. It may be physically made around you, perhaps with items or objects that are significant, candles, salt, or even just a circle drawn around you. Other times, it is entirely comprised of energy, and no one else will see it.

This has two key functions: It protects you—you prevent negative energies from feeding upon you or taking the place of the positive energy that you are expending, and it contains your energy—it allows for you to regulate the flow of your energy and magnify it. When you are ready to cast your circle, you will follow six simple steps—if you do them all properly, you should feel the circle build up around you.

- **Step 1:** Identify where you will set up your circle—ideally, it is flat and open, and you will not be bothered.

- **Step 2:** Identify the four cardinal directions—either by knowing your surroundings or by using your phone or any other compass that you may have on hand.

- **Step 3:** With your cardinal directions, you need to set up representations for the Elements on the circle that you are imagining, or that you have traced around you. For most people that are alone, this is quite small, maybe 5 feet across. At the northernmost point, represent earth. At the easternmost point, represent air. At the southernmost point, represent fire. At the westernmost point, represent water. If you are unsure what to use as representations, try the following:

  - **Earth (North):** Crystals or rocks, a plant in a pot, ceramics.
  - **Air (East):** Sage burning, a stick of incense burning, or a feather.
  - **Fire (South):** A candle, a tea light, and essential oil burner.

- **Water (West):** A cup or bowl with water, a seashell, scales from a fish.

- **Step 4:** Face the east while standing in the middle of the circle. Take a deep, grounding breath and breathe until you feel like you are relaxed and entering a state of mindfulness. At this point, imagine the air around you, focusing on the element itself and tuning into it. Call upon the air as you feel that connection—try saying, "I call upon the Spirits of Air," or some other variation of this.

Turn south now. Think about fire and the warmth it brings as it burns. As you allow yourself to relate to the flames, call upon the Spirits of Fire as well.

Now, turn west. Imagine water, allowing yourself to become in tune with the very element itself—perhaps you can feel the flow of the water around you. Call upon the

Spirits of Water.

Lastly, turn north. Think of the scent of petrichor—the smell of a rainy day. Imagine the feeling of a sturdy mountain beneath your feet, and allow yourself to connect to the earth. Call upon the Spirits of Earth.

While facing north, focus on your feet—imagine yourself projecting energy, like roots, down into the earth, and envision yourself drawing up light energy from the Earth's core. Call upon Mother Earth.

Now imagine that same energy that you envisioned as roots entering the ground and send it up into the sky. Shoot it out into space as far as it can go from your head, and feel it returning back to you. Call upon Father Sky.

Allow yourself to feel fully protected and armed against negativity and thank the

Deities for providing for you. Voice these thanks with something along the lines of, "Thank you, the circle is cast. Blessed be."

- **Step 5:** Now, meditate in the circle, or choose now to cast your spell.

- **Step 6:** When you are done using the circle, it is time to release it. Do this through thanking the Earth, the Sky, and each element. Face the direction that corresponded to the element, imagine that element in your mind, feeling the connection fondly and acknowledge its presence. "Thank you, water; I acknowledge that you were   here."

After thanking each element, Mother Earth, and Father Sky, thank everyone as a group—use three thanks, followed by, "Blessed be. And so, it is." Now wait a moment before speaking once more: "I open the circle, yet it is unbroken. The Goddess's love lives on in my heart forever. We meet, we part, and we meet again." Imagine that the energy is released into the world at this point, and you are done!

Setting Up An Altar

Another common term you will run into while preparing spells is the altar—this is a space that is sacred and reserved for connections to the God and Goddess—when you use your altar, you may be meditating, or casting a spell or ritual. You may even be praying. No matter what you are doing, you will find yourself at it often, so make sure it is comfortable.

First, make sure you know whether you wish for it to be inside or outside—people have different preferences. If your climate is not conducive to this, you could instead decide to make an indoor altar. Alternatively, you could set up your altar to allow for portability. If it is indoors, choose somewhere private, where you know that you will not be interrupted.

Next, you must choose the direction for your altar—most often, they are facing the east because that is the direction in which the sun rises. However, some people choose to face north simply because many spells start in the north. You may instead choose to face the direction of your element.

Now, choose your preference for placement. This can be somewhere permanent, such as on a dresser in your room, on a shelf, or even a table. Some people may use a drawer in their dresser or a windowsill. If you are outside, you may choose to use a tree stump or a large, mostly flat stone. If you are short on space, you may instead choose to place your items within a box and pull them out when you will use them and put them away afterward. Particularly if you have young children that may damage your items or may be at risk of hurting themselves on your items, putting them away, maybe for the best.

With your location secured, you can now choose the style in which you are choosing to use. You may choose symbolism from whichever beliefs you feel resonate with you, or you may instead choose to make it entirely personal to you without following any particular pattern. Remember, this is *your* alter for *your* personal beliefs—you can choose to set this up in any way you see fit.

Now, traditionally, you would choose an item or items to represent the Goddess—she represents the Moon itself. You may choose to use a candle, a statue that shows a Moon goddess, or whichever seems to resonate with you. You could choose to use some sort of totem animal that you feel relates to the Goddess as well, or something that you can represent with femininity.

Next, choose the items that are representative of the God for you. This is the Sun—you can use anything that represents the God for you, such as candles, statues, masculine elements (fire and air).

In the center of your altar, you will choose to place something that resonates with you—some people choose a primary deity. Others may choose to place something reminiscent of the element of Aether (spirit). You may even choose to place a pentacle or your Book of Shadows. The pentacle is typically on the Goddess side of the altar while the Athame or wand may go on the God side.

At this point, you can add anything else you feel may be important to include—crystals, herbs, a box, objects for spells, amulets, charms, or anything else that really feels like it needs to be included.

Other Tools You Need To Know

The choice of tools that are used is largely dependent upon the person practicing magic at any given moment. These different tools vary greatly, and you should choose those that you think that you will use regularly. Nevertheless, this section will give you a list of commonly used tools.

- **The Chalice:** a goblet or cup that is representative of the Goddess and water. It represents fertility and is frequently used to hold water, ale, wine, or even remained empty sometimes.

- **The Wand:** A piece of wood under the length of one foot—it may be made from pewter sometimes, or have gemstones attached, though most prefer wood from the willow, alder, hazel, or oak trees. This is representative of both the God and Goddess, used as a way to direct and project energy, and it can be affixed to either the element of fire or air.

- **The Pentacle:** A round coin or other sort of slab with magical symbols etched into it. Usually, it is the pentagram, which is the five-point star with a circle around it. This is representative of Earth.

- **The Athame:** (A-tha-mae) A ritual knife that is double-edged. It directs energy and cuts the ties between energies. It is not usually very sharp due to the fact that it does not actually cut physical items. It is representative of God, and can be bonded to either fire or air.

- **The Censer:** Allows for the burn of incense.

- **Candles:** These can be burned for a representation of the fire element and also can be used to represent the God and Goddess.

- **The Broom:** Not necessarily used in rituals, the broom is used to cleanse the area, purifying the energies, or closing a circle.

- **The Cauldron:** Not crucial to rituals, but it works well as a place to hold burning candles or other items that must be burnt to keep a fire-safe indoors. It may also be used to scry when filled with water, or to brew potions.

- **The Bell:** Not essential, but still a good tool to know and understand, the bell's tone is meant to be cleansing, pushing out negative energy, or even just clearing out an empty room's neutral energy to allow for positive to enter. Usually, this is associated with the Goddess and the element of air, held on the left side of the altar.

Chapter 8: 33 Magical Spells Of A Lunar Grimoire

And now, it is time—you are going to get several different spells that will help you in the beginning journey into Wicca. As you read through this chapter, remember to keep in mind the cycle of the Moon for the best results. If you want your spells to really make a difference in the world, you want to make sure that they align with the Moon's phase.

Using The Energy Of The Moon

The Moon, as the only body naturally circling the Earth at the moment, is always present. It is always nearby, always influencing the flow of energies on the Earth. It influences everything from the weather and natural disasters all the way to fertility, as has been discussed.

When practicing magic, then, you can tap into this power with ease. You can ensure that you utilize the energy, the influence, and the ability to act upon the world around you as well. Those practicing Wicca have become particularly skilled at this, recognizing the ebb and flow of energy and how certain spells seem to work best during specific periods and phases of the Moon.

Casting Spells During The New Moon

During the New Moon, you want to focus primarily on goal-setting and preparative spellcasting. By doing so, you can make sure that you are ready for anything that comes in the future phases. Remember, the power is at the strongest in the Full Moon, and it is when the New Moon arrives that we send our intentions into the world, using the energy from the Moon as she transforms from the Infant to the Maiden and then to the Mother. This period of growth begins with the Moon being entirely invisible, known as a Dark Moon, and then begins to appear.

During this stage, you want to set up your intentions—this is the beginning of the Lunar Cycle, and you want to hit it off on the right foot. You may clean up your altar and home, or choose to meditate or cleanse yourself.

Road Opener Spell

This spell is designed to direct your intention toward figuring out how to get through a problem—it is an attempt to get past an obstacle and instead work toward solving the problem altogether. This spell requires little more than ingredients that are most likely already sitting in your kitchen as you read through this. You need a representative of each of the major elements: Earth, water, fire, and air.

In this instance, take a bowl of water, a crystal or gemstone (or substitute a bowl filled with salt if you do not have one) for earth, an incense stick to represent air, and a candle to burn to represent fire. Make sure that the incense you choose matches your intention, or even lines up with the moon in which you are working at this moment.

Arrange everything onto your altar, with each element facing a different direction. Start with earth at the northern point of the altar with fire to the south, water to the west, and air to the east. Light up your incense, and as you do this, you bring air into your ritual—acknowledge its presence.

Rub your hands together now as you breathe in the incense around you. As you feel warmth building within your palms, imagine it forming a ball in your hand and pick up your crystal, or place your hand within the bowl of salt. This is an invocation of the earth.

Now, you will light up your candle—doing so immediately invokes fire.

Place one finger gently into the water—feel the water around you. In this spell, water is pertinent to success—it will help you flow, allowing you to effectively clear out your mind to push past any and all blockages that may be present at the moment.

It is time to chant your prayer, speaking out your intentions for the Universe.

"By the Elements of the Universal Light,
I call upon thee to lend me your strength.
Open the paths before me and watch as I go.
I trust your guidance, so mote it be."

As you do this, imagine that you are on a road that is entirely empty, devoid of all life and of anyone other than the road in front of you, before you finally move down it. Allow the candle to keep burning as you do this, imagining the process of moving down the road the entire time.

As the candle finishes burning, clean up the mess and say thank you, making sure you keep your crystal on your person.

This will help you feel like you can get past whatever it is that is holding you back at that moment in time.

You will get past mental blocks or reservations, coming up with the best possible solution.

Peace Spell

To cast your peace spell, you want to evoke the energies of peace and calmness. In doing so, you are allowing yourself to evoke the feeling of confidence and that you will be able to find a solution to whatever problem is causing you anguish at that moment in time.

When you wish to start this spell, set up a space with calming music. Choose a comfortable position to sit, either on the floor or in a chair. You will be placing candles around you, so make sure that wherever you are, it is not a fire risk.

Take a deep inhale and exhale, tensing up your muscles as you inhale and then releasing the tension at the exhale. Do these three times, feeling the air move within your body.

Now, light the candles as you go in a clockwise manner around the outside of the circle. As you finish lighting them, take a deep breath, returning your focus to your diaphragm as you breathe in and out. Imagine that there is light in your abdomen, visualizing it and feeling its warmth as it emanates outward, slowly making its way to your extremities.

During this visualization, imagine the light bringing with its purity, serenity, and the peace of mind that you were seeking. Stay in this position, with this feeling emanating within you until you are satisfied or your candles burn out. When you are done, make sure you blow out all of the candles.

Spiritual Protection Spell

This spell will work to eliminate negativity and evil from home, cleaning the home from evil and creating purity. In eliminating any evil spirits or negative energies, then, you are able to keep your home happier in general. There will be less stress, and you will feel more at ease.

This spell works with two simple ingredients—you will use coarse salt and a broom, along with some chanting. The salt will purify the area, sending away the spirits in the room and cleansing the energy. It is a good idea to first start with your normal broom that you use to clean the room that you are using, rather than your broom dedicated to your magic— this way you can make sure your room is clean before you do the spiritual cleanse and protection.

Then, spread the coarse salt across the floor, using your ritual broom (if you have one—your normal one will suffice if you do not) to spread the salt across the ground, covering the entire room. As you do so, repeat:

"While I sweep this salt with my broom,
I banish all spirits from this room."

Repeat this from time to time before finally sweeping all of the salt into a dustpan. When you get it swept up, dump the salt into the toilet and flush, asking for the element of water to pull away the negative energy and allow for the finishing of the purification.

Good Luck Spell

Luck is something that people think is entirely random—some people are more or less lucky. However, this is wrong—luck is more than that. Luck is having the right attitude to begin with rather than feeling like you have no choice but to be tossed around by chance. Within this spell, you will learn how to tap into luck.

To make yourself luckier, all you need to do is develop the necessary self-confidence. This brings along the success that you will find. On the other hand, those who feel down on themselves tend to attract bad energy, and therefore attract bad luck.

This spell will utilize salt to purify, rose petals as an offering, and the New Moon present to energize you and bring the good luck flowing toward you in no time.

When you want to do this spell to attract good luck, you start by placing a dish upon your altar. With a handful of salt, create a circle on the dish. Then, take the seven petals from the red rose and place them atop the salt circle. In the center of the circle, you must place your white candle and light it.

With the candlelit, you then sit and relax, breathing as slowly as you can manage comfortably. Imagine how your life clears out around you, giving you space for positive energy and intentions to flow inwards, opening the doors to peace and prosperity.

Now, give thanks to the universe and repeat a positive intention, such as:

"I only welcome positive energy and good luck into my life."

Then, meditate for at least ten minutes, focusing on exactly how you will find that the good luck is manifesting around you. Repeat this process for a week.

Protection Spell

Sometimes, what you need to do is to create the circle of protection around you. When you do this, you essentially are making sure that you surround yourself with enough energy that you can protect yourself from negativity. Doing so involves creating a circle of protection, invoking the elements, and using the energy from them to ward away evil or negative energy.

To begin, identify the space that you will work within, creating a circle that is big enough for you to reach out and will have all of the space necessary to accommodate for moving around and making sure that you can complete any spell work you will do. You can mark this with chalk, dirt, salt, or stones, or you may choose instead to remember where your boundaries lie and leave it unmarked.

Clean the area, sweeping the space to remove the negative energy within the circle that you will be using. Along with sweeping, some people have luck with lighting incense, spreading salt, or even using a bell's chimes to ward off negativity.

Now, prepare your altar—make sure that you bring anything with you that you will be needing. Set up the altar and place down candles at each of the four cardinal points are.

Next, it is time to draw your circle—you can use a tool for this, such as an athame or a wand if you have one, but if not, you can use your finger just as easily. As you do this, take a deep breath, and imagine the energy welling up within you; with each breath, it gets larger and larger, threatening to spill over and out into the world. However, instead, you direct the energy, guiding it through your arm and into your tool or hand that you are using. Envision that energy settling around you, along the path of the circle you are creating.

For some people, they like to involve several circles, but that is up to personal preference. If once is enough for you, that is fine. You then have the option to invoke the elements, setting the elements on their respective sides, and representing the elements. From there, you ask the God and Goddess to bless your circle to protect you.

"I ask the God and Goddess to bless this circle. Within it is a safe zone in which I am sheltered and free."

Now, all that is left to do is open the circle—you will do this by turning in the opposite direction that you went through to set the original circle in the first place. This should neutralize the outline you had made prior. Thank the elements and Deities for guiding and empowering you, and you are done.

Casting Spells During The Waxing Crescent Moon

The Waxing Crescent Moon involves the three days after the birth of the New Moon—you can see a sliver of the moon in the sky, though the vast majority of it is hidden. When you are casting spells during the Waxing Crescent Moon, you will be best served focusing on money and career spells as well as the creating of Moon water. Doing so can help you grow the career or money that you are attempting to bless, just as the moon will continue to grow and swell through the cycle.

7-Day Money Spell

This spell is quite simple—it involves visualization and focus, and if you can do so, you should be able to attract the wealth you are seeking in your life. All you will need for this spell is a single green candle, a single candle holder, or a plate or other dish if you do not have one, a piece of paper, and a pen.

First, start by drawing the symbol for your currency, whether your currency is in dollars, pounds, euros, or something entirely different altogether. Spend a few moments decorating your drawing of your money symbol, focusing on the image of the money sign and relaxing as you draw.

After the few minutes are up, write down how much money you need—but make sure it is something realistic. It NEEDS to be money that you can realistically attain. Now, visualize it in your bank account. Imagine seeing the transaction and the new available balance.

Place your candle into the candle holder with your paper that has been decorated placed underneath the candle holder, and light it. Now, for the next fifteen minutes, imagine that you are receiving the money, visualizing it arriving somehow. Maybe it flies in on the wind, or it is given to you by a family member, or maybe you win the lottery. The most important part is to imagine that it is coming to you, rather than focusing on how it will get there. Simply trust that it will. As your candle continues to burn, meditate on the images, and watch as the wax drips to cover the paper. It does not have to saturate or entirely coat the paper, but it does need to at least touch it somewhat.

As soon as you have gotten wax on the paper, blow out the candle and move on. Every day, for the next week, repeat this cycle, using the same candle on the same paper at the same time. At the very end, on day 7, take your original paper and burn it. You should see the money arriving shortly if you do it right.

Fresh Funds Basil Spell

This is another fund attracting spell, this time utilizing kitchen magick—particularly basil. Basil itself, interestingly enough, comes from the Greek word for royal. This herb, then, even back in ancient times, was linked to royalty. This is important to consider—it is going to be used then for all sorts of magic meant to bring about money and prosperity.

Beyond the basil, you will also use garlic, which will create the added protection that will safeguard against the negative intentions in life. You will use one bill of your local currency, preferably one of the largest bills, essential oils of your choice, and a white handkerchief.

Lastly, you need a "hoodoo box"—this is any sort of box, with or without a lock. In a pinch, you can use a shoebox.

First, place the bill within the box. Atop that bill, you need to set the head of garlic. It does not need to be cut or anything—just placed atop the bill. Then, chant out the following:

"It's time, it's time,
to connect and combine.
This timeless magic, fresh allure,
Increase funds and stay secure."

After the chant, place the basil leaves atop the bill with the garlic, and cover the whole thing with a white handkerchief. At that, place a few drops of oil onto the cloth. Cinnamon oil is a great one in this instance.

Now, close the box or chest and set it under your bed. Money should come in time. You should allow it to sit under your bed for one entire cycle, so at least 28 days without being touched.

Ocean Charm

Using this spell will attract money through the use of sea salt, seashells, candles, and incense. Salt itself has a myriad of uses—it can be used to cleanse, protect, purify, and attract good luck as well, making it a fantastic choice when it comes to inviting or attracting certain aspects into your life.

This spell will work due to the cleansing Earth element of sea salt. Seashells then will provide the element of water, representing the power that the ocean wields. The green candles are meant to attract the money while the white candle acts as a protector, tapping into the element of fire. Lastly, the incense stick invites the energy of the element air.

Start by placing a dish in the center of the altar you are using, and then place all three candles, the white and green. Light the incense, using any essence that you choose in this stage.

Next, use your seashells between the candles, decorating the dish, or right around it. This can be in any pattern with as many as you want or as few as you want—you are in control. Go with your gut reaction.

Now, you want to make a circle with the salt, ensuring that the circle encompasses everything on and around the dish. At this point, light the candles and focus as much as you can, directing your energy all toward what you are attracting—in this case, money. Focus on how much money you need, and think about exactly why it is needed in the first place as well.

Imagine that you are getting what you want, feeling the emotions that you would associate with them. You may imagine feeling satisfied at achieving your need, or the excitement of getting the money. Focus on those feelings, directing them toward the candles on the altar. With one more handful of salt along the shells, it is time to chant:

"Thank you, the Elements within this vast Universe,
for communing with me, providing
and gifting me the beautiful gift of life itself.
My life is successful and prosperous in money and wealth.
I feel successful in all of my endeavors and I walk a path of prosperity.
I am in perfect peace, perfect exactly how it is.
So, mote it be."

Allow the candles to burn as you meditate, and then dispose of the wax and salt, preferably in a source of water, or buried in the earth if you can. If neither of those are options, then dispose of them accordingly in the trash. The seashells, however, should remain in your room, somewhere that you see regularly.

Money Bag Cinnamon Spell

Yet another spell that you can use to invite prosperity to your home once and for all is creating money bags—these work quite simply. You will use a green candle, coins, cinnamon, green cloth, prosperity oil, and string to create bags that will attract prosperity into your life.

Start with all ingredients placed upon your altar and take some cleansing breaths. You need to make sure that your own mind is perfectly clear for this process. Prepare your candle by rubbing the oil you have chosen to represent your prosperity. All you will do to do so is rub oil onto your fingers, and then onto the candle itself, focusing your intention on attracting money.

Place the candle into a candle holder that should be waiting atop the alter at the moment, and then surround the candle with six coins. Imagine yourself having received any money that you needed and imagine the thankfulness that you felt at having received it. Project that gratitude straight into the coins as you chant three times:

"Money grows and Money flows,
Money, multiply.
Allow abundance to reflect on me
And on all that is currently mine."

After reciting the spell three times, place the cloth onto the altar and sprinkle your cinnamon across the top. Now take each of the coins and say:

"Money, Money,
Come to me
Harm no one
So, mote it be."

You should recite this with every coin that you pick up and set down onto your cloth covered in cinnamon. Now, take the corners of the cloth and create a sachet, tying it with a small piece of string. Now, carry this amulet with you wherever you go, in a bag, pocket, or purse. At any point that you are interacting with your bag, make sure you envision having the money that you hope to attract.

Silver Moon Money Spell

This is the last of the money spells for now—you are going to need a cauldron, a single quarter, and water in order to manifest and attract more money into your life with ease.

Effectively, you will charge water under the Moon and then use the water to charge the quarter. While this is traditionally done during a Full Moon, doing so during any Moon phase other than the Full Moon will still show some effect.

Fill your cauldron up with water—if you do not have a cauldron, any other bowl or pot will work as well. Place the quarter into the water as well and then set the entire cauldron onto a table or outside where the Moonlight will have the chance to reflect upon it. As you set it down, say the following thrice:

"Good, Just Moon,

Your Will and my desires are always in tune.
Line my pockets with silver and gold,
So, anything I may need, I can then afford."

With the spell repeated, leave the water in the Moonlight. The next morning, you can take the quarter out of the cauldron or pot and use the water to water a flower or other plant in your area. Place the quarter in your wallet for a week, carrying it with you everywhere, and after a week, spend it somewhere, releasing it, and therefore your intentions, back into the Universe.

Casting Spell During The First Quarter Moon

The First Quarter Moon is perfect for any of the spells regarding love, luck, or healing—during this period, the Moon is still swelling up, reaching about the halfway mark before the Moon begins to swell toward the Full Moon of the Mother. This period of time is roughly 7 days after the arrival of the New Moon—it is the perfect time to address self-healing and growth as well. Just as the energies of the Moon are ramping up, you can start to use them yourself to help yourself to grow as well.

Remember, this phase of the Moon is quite charged—you should focus mostly upon your own introspection. Try to stick to easier, beginner's spells, such as the ones that are listed here.

Bad Luck Repeller Spell

This spell works by harnessing its ingredients (one green candle, cinnamon, and salt) and casting a double-intentioned good luck spell. This means, then, that it is going to be similar to the good luck spell you learned earlier in this chapter, except this time, you will use two intentions instead of just one, using the salt and candle to purify while the cinnamon then purifies the energy flowing back toward you.

First, you will stand your candle atop your altar, positioned in the center. Take your salt, make a circle around the candle, and say:

"I'll fortune, I demand that you leave me now."

Light up the candle at this point and say:

"All struggles now dissolve."

As you speak these words, imagine all of the bad luck that has been plaguing your life as of recently—imagine it all spreading throughout your life and dissipating as you do so. It should gather as you focus on the candle, and you can then expel it.

Now, imagine that your problems are all fading away around you—you are somehow overcoming them and they are becoming nonissues. Meditate on this, focusing on the imagery. Stay in this meditative state for at least five minutes.

After the five minutes end, sprinkle some of your cinnamon atop the salt, uttering:

"I only welcome good luck and positive energy within me now."

As you assert this, imagine that all of the energy that is flowing your way within the universe is positive, bright, powerful, and meaningful. Let the good intentions and feelings flow inwards to you, drowning out any of the negative and bad thoughts and memories. As you think and reflect upon the good new opportunities in the future, allow the candle to finish burning.

Magic Armor Spell

This spell is incredibly simple to pull off—all you need to do is use four ingredients, allowing you to create the protection you desire. You will need salt, which is naturally purifying and protecting—it used to be used to preserve food when refrigeration was not possible, and because of the protection that it allowed for, it has become well-known as being protective. You will need an onion—these used to be used to provide strength and health, and have several uses in health, career, and divination spells. You will need a white candle—this represents the purity you need, as well as the God and Goddess. Lastly, you will need a photo of you, or if you do not have one easily available, using your name written on paper is also sufficient.

Start by lighting your candle on your altar. With your photo (or paper with your name) next to the candle, take the onion and place it atop the paper. Now create a salt circle around the candle and paper or photo.

Focus on the flame above for a few moments, taking in a deep breath as you watch it flicker. Close your eyes as you exhale and begin to meditate, focusing on yourself before chanting the following:

"By the Powers of Nature,
Allow the Winds to come to me.
May this sacred circle surround and protect me.
May the flickering of this flame enlighten me.

Allow the waters of the Earth to guide me.
So, mote it be."

After reciting the spell, meditate further for a few moments, keeping your breathing even.

When you are done, blow out the candle and bury the candle and onion into the earth—either a flowerpot or a garden. Make sure you hold onto the photo, keeping it safe.

Fire Flower Love Spell

This will be your first introduction to love spells—as intimidating as this may sound, do not worry! You are merely sending good vibrations into the universe with your intentions, imploring for them to be answered, but you are not forcing anyone into anything at all. This spell works similarly to the road opener spell—you use this spell to open up those who have closed themselves off due to a traumatic relationship or breakup in the past. This enables them to open themselves once more to love.

This spell will utilize easy to find ingredients—a pink candle to relieve any anxiety that surrounds love, incense, three white flowers, and an essential oil. The best pick for an essential oil would be something uplifting and light—perhaps cinnamon, yarrow, vanilla, rose, orange, or jasmine. A few others would work too, such as linden flower, myrtle, or palmarosa. Take your pick. You will then require a fireproof container, such as your cauldron, paper, and a writing utensil, and a candle holder.

Start by lighting your incense, allowing the scent to waft throughout the room. As you do this, dress the candle—remember, this means that you are rubbing oil along it as you transfer your intentions to the candle. At this step, say:

"I am consecrating this candle so that it may be the sign of the sacred covenant between myself and the Fire."

Now, with the candle dressed, light it and set it into its dish or holder. You will then take one flower, gently plucking off the petals one at a time. Now you will use your breathing in tandem with the following chant:

"I am (breathe in)
Filled to the brim with power (breathe out)
A passionate love (breathe in)
That blazes like fire (breathe out)."

Repeat this process as you move through all three flowers, plucking the petals and placing them within the cauldron. Take a brief moment to clear your mind before moving forward. You will then write your entire name on your paper—first, middle, and last name. Dip the corner of your paper into the candle's flame in order to ignite it and then gently place it within the cauldron to burn safely with the rose petals. Now, you wait, meditating on your process as the candle continues to burn. When it burns out, bury the candle's remains while giving thanks to the fire element, and then take the ashes and petals from the cauldron and bury them as well.

Self-Love Renewal Spell

This spell involves renewing your self-love, teaching you to accept your body exactly as it is These spells work well at any point, but they are especially potent during this period. You will need cinnamon, which will heal your energy, rose petals to encourage love, and the use of a positive affirmation. You can choose to add in candles and incense if you would like the ambiance, but none of that is necessarily required.

First, begin by placing four cups of water into a pot, bringing it to a boil on the stove burner over high heat. Toss in the rose petals and the cinnamon, waiting for it to boil. As soon as you start to see bubbling and boiling, turn off the heat and allow the water to steep for 15 minutes.

During that time, go shower, cleaning dirt and oils off of your body to prepare for a bathing ritual. You want to be clean before you get into the cleansing bath. With the shower complete, fill up the tub with warm water that is comfortable for you. Light a candle to help harness energy, and then mix the brew from your stovetop into the water.

Now, get into the tub and bathe in the water. Pour it over your face and reflect on what is hurting you right now. Do not worry about what other people are thinking or feeling; instead, look at how you are thinking and feeling about yourself. For each and every negative thought that you have come up for you during your reflection, you must apologize before banishing the negativity. Instead of allowing yourself to dwell on the negatives, instead analyze why you are afraid, trusting your intuition. At this point, you can say:

"I love myself completely and wholly.
From here on out,
I accept who I am and
Challenge all negative thoughts."

As you chant to yourself, encouraging yourself to accept yourself for who you are once and for all, relax and spend as much time as you think is necessary within the tub. When you do get out, treat yourself to something you love—this could be art, reading, or even enjoying a sweet treat, so long as it brings you joy. This will help fight off the negativity and bring back to you the positive nature and feelings you need.

Forget the Ex Spell

This next spell is used to help you move on from a bad relationship that you simply cannot move on from. This spell will require you to meditate, along with using a photo of yourself, a white candle, a glass jar with water, and a single tsp of olive oil. The meditation will help you push past your feelings and unblock your mind.

First, you must place your photograph onto the altar in front of you, or on a table or floor if an altar is not available to you. Place your jar of water atop the photo. You should be able to see your photograph through it. Now, pour the olive oil into the water and place the candle right behind the jar. Light the candle and recite:

"Calling upon the power of the Sacred Elements,
I undo everything that ties me to
[Ex's full name here]. I relinquish it
And let it go.
With the strength of my soul, I proclaim that
This relationship is over, and I allow
[Ex's full name here] to follow his/her path.
I trust my fate to the God and Goddess, so
I can find my own inner peace and balance.
I push myself toward a future of joy and
Happiness above everything else. So, mote it be."

With that said, meditate, and focus on allowing yourself to release everything about the individual that you are trying to forget. Instead of allowing your mind to wander to your own heartbreak, you are effectively forcing your mind to see your own good, particularly if you use this along with the self-love ritual.

When the candle burns out, dump the water into the sink and dispose of the candle. Your photograph should not be thrown away. Keep in mind that this sometimes requires a few repetitions to really help. If you persevere, you will heal.

Casting Spell During The Waxing Gibbous Moon

The Waxing Gibbous Moon is the fourth of the Moon phases—it is from the 10th day after the New Moon for three days. During this time, the universe's power is swelling and taking control. During this stage, it is time to be patient. If you have cast a spell somewhere during the Moon phase, allow it to continue to grow and swell with the Moon. This stage is best served with spells that encourage observations and reflections.

Peace of Mind Spell

This spell involves you overcoming fear or uncertainty, allowing yourself to finally release that fear that is holding you back. This stage involves the lighting of candles, the playing of ambient music, and the use of spiritual cleansing herbal water, all together to create peace of mind, even if just temporarily.

Start by showering to clean yourself with soap and water—this prepares you for your bath. Then, move on to boiling water on the stove, adding the herbs that you will need to use. You can try salt and lavender oil, or even rue, rosemary, and guinea hen weed to really up the ante on the bath's effects on your peace of mind. Allow the herbs to boil, then strain them.

Pour the herbs into the bathwater, and surround the edge of your tub with candles. Moving in a clockwise manner, light all of the candles, focusing on your breathing as you do so. Enter the bath and let yourself soak before focusing your attention on your breathing. Imagine that you are pulling in good intentions from the ground and air, firing away the negative as you do so. Rest in the herbal bath as the candles burn, meditating and visualizing to find the peace within yourself.

Herbal Aura Cleansing Spell

If you have been feeling particularly caught up in negative mindsets recently, you may just need a spiritual bath—this sort of herbal aura cleansing should have you doing better in no time. This works because rue, one of the herbs, promotes optimism. Rosemary encourages healing and self-love. Guinea hen weed is an antioxidant which allows it to help relieve pain and fight off any bacteria that may be the root of your problems.

Using a spring of rue, a spring of rosemary, and three guinea hen weed leaves, boil four cups of water on the stove for 30 minutes. As these boils, go take a normal shower, washing yourself from dirt and oils. When the water is prepped, prepare a bath as well, filling the tub with water at a comfortable temperature. Then, light a candle on the counter and return to your herbal solution. Remove the herbs, filtering the water into its own container, and then return to the bathroom.

Keeping your mixture in a separate container, take water with your hands from the jar and rub it onto yourself. As you do so, imagine that your body is pushing away the negative energy, it is being pulled away with the solution as you clean yourself. Every time you feel like you have unearthed an important feeling, analyze, and reflect on it before releasing it.

Upon finishing, allow the water to drain and imagine all of the negativity you have purified from your body disappearing down the drain once and for all, and air dry.

As one quick note—make sure you avoid this spell if you are currently pregnant—Guinea hen weed should be avoided during pregnancy.

Anti-Stress Tea Spell

The next spell you will be introduced for is a calming spell, allowing you to utilize the power of Hyssop tea while meditating. Hyssop is naturally sedative—it will relax your body and between that and the visualization and guided meditation, you should start to feel the stress melt away.

You will first start by brewing your tea—boil some water while turning off any and all electronics—yes, even the device you are reading this on right now! Take a deep breath and begin to relax as you wait for the water to boil. When it does, add the tea leaves to your mug—one tea bag of Hyssop tea or approximately one tablespoon of loose leaves if that happens to be what you have on hand. Pour the hot water into your cup and leave it to steep. As you wait, light a blue candle, and relax.

Sip at your tea and try playing a guided meditation in which you can follow along as you relax. This should melt away your stress.

One more quick note is needed here—if you are going to treat yourself with the consumption of herbs, always speak to your doctor if you are already taking a prescription or if you are pregnant or breastfeeding.

Spiritual Delight Bath

Sometimes, what you need to boost yourself spiritually is a healing bath. This bath, in particular, will utilize salt and lavender oil—salt is purifying and lavender is important as an antiseptic.

The steps to this particular spell are simple—fill up a hot bath at a temperature you know will be comfortable, and then add one cup of coarse salt—either sea salt or Epsom salt will work best here. Then, add in ten drops of lavender essential oil. Using your hand, mix up the water in order to dissolve the salt, and get into the water.

You should try to soak for at least 30 minutes, absorbing all of the benefits of lavender and salt with ease. As you do so, try repeating this chant:

"I am cleansing myself of any vanity;
I am removing from myself discontent;
I free my body of its ego;
I fill myself with self-respect."

As you recite this, as much as you feel is necessary, imagine that your problems are fading away around you—literally melting away with little effort. Finally, when the bath chills or you are done, get up and allow the saltwater, which should have absorbed all of your negativity be swept away.

House Cleansing Spell

Next, it is time to cleans the house—you spend so much time in your house that purifying it is absolutely essential. Make sure that you utilize both sage and Palo Santo—these are two herbs that you can burn to purify the soul. Palo Santo is burned to balance energy and promote harmony, while sage is a disinfectant and encourages intelligence and wisdom.

Start this process by preparing your altar and set a white candle next to your cauldron. Light the Palo Santo and place it within the cauldron to burn, and do the same with the smudge stick of sage as well. While the smoke fills the room, light your white candle as well before chanting:

"The Goddess of the Earth and the Celestial Dome, True is my Heart, and clear may be my home."

As you do this, you invite positive energy as the negative energy is all pushed away.

Repeat this process as much as you feel is necessary and allow the smoke to fill the room until the candle finally burns out.

Casting Spell During The Full Moon

Remember, the Moon's energy is at its strongest during the Full Moon—this is two weeks after the New Moon, and it is impossible to miss on a clear night—this Moon is all about communication and interaction—it is romantic, and you will find your spell powers bolstered. During this stage, you can cast any spell that you desire—however, this section will address a handful that is specific to the Full Moon's light.

Lunar Protection Spell

This spell is a simple kitchen spell—it uses cloves that will encourage the development of production and mental clarity, while the sage serves to purify. Start this process by filling a bowl with water and setting it on your altar with a white candle next to it. Light the candle and then burn some sage incense or a smudge stick next to it. Add some cloves to your water as the candle and sage continue to burn. During this time, allow yourself to focus on

the protective powers of the universe and the sage
that you are breathing inward. Imagine a shield all
around you and say:

*"I welcome the shielding powers of the Lord and
Lady,*
To envelope me in a formidable Fire shield.
*To imbue in me the strength and grace of the
Earth.*
*Along the Winds comes my wisdom, and the Water
brings me Fortune.*
*I release my anxieties and worries so I can remain
in touch with the pulse of Life.*
*Allow this under the Moon, and for the best interest
of All.*
So be it, so it shall be."

As the candle burns, meditate on the words you
have spoken and release energy back to the
Universe, at which point you can put out the candle.

Full Moon Love Spell

This spell draws upon the power of the Full Moon, and even better—it is ingredient-free! All you need is yourself and the light of the Moon. This works through viewing the Moon's light as an inspiration, allowing it to fill you with confidence.

Start by finding a comfortable place to sit outside. Stare up at the moon as you do so, imagining her light, her energy reaching out toward you. Imagine that you are bathing in her energy before turning your attention to the one you love. As you do so, raise your arms up to the sky as you take in a deep breath.

Hold the air before slowly releasing it, gently lowering, and resting your hands onto your lap. Place one hand on top of the other and speak the following:

"Dear Moon, Mother and Sister,
Through your feminine energy

I summon your power.
Through the force of your light,
Allow him/her to come closer."

Breathe deeply as you continue to think about the other person as you meditate under the light of the Moon. As you do so, let her light fill you with confidence. When you are feeling more confident, head back inside. Repeat these three nights in a row and reap the benefits.

Lust & Passion Spell

This spell is meant to instill desire back into your relationship—particularly for partners and spouses more so than attracting someone that you do not yet have a relationship with. This is perfect for when you know the other person still loves you but you feel like the passion is lacking. It works by taking red candles, reminiscent of passion, and burning them with incantations as they burn, combining the sweetness from the sugar and honey with the photograph.

Start this ritual underneath the full moon—preferably with your partner together with you. At your altar, place four candles together, creating a square, and light them. Place the photo of the two of you inside of a glass container and place both honey and sugar into the container as well before placing the glass into the center.

Together, you should both say:

*"Destiny pulled us together,
True love endures forever."*

This should be repeated seven times before blowing out the candles and then place the glass container, with the photo, somewhere no one else will find them. You want to make sure you save the candles, container, and photo and use them, repeating this ritual weekly for 28 days. During the last burn, you can let the candles burn themselves out.

Job Security Spell

This spell will work to secure your job, taking the energy from the Moon and imbuing them into your clothes and home—doing so then allows you to protect yourself from potentially losing your job. All you will need to complete this ritual is to have a bowl of Full Moon water, which will be addressed shortly.

In order to complete this spell, take a bowl filled with Full Moon water and place your clothing on your bed, with the water next to you. Using your fingers dipped into the Moon water, sprinkle the droplets of water across the clothing while saying:

"Guard and protect me from the Evil Eye.
Imbue me with illuminating, cleansing light.
May only good people come my way,
With gentleness and care during my workday."

While reciting this, imagine how many good things will happen throughout the day. Smile as you thank yourself and the Moon for her energy and blessing.

Full Moon Money Attraction Spell

This spell is all about enhancing the Full Moon's magic to take advantage of attracting money. This spell will use sugar, which is primarily meant to be a sweetener for love spells, but in this case, it will be used as an offering to the Moon. Water, then, will absorb and channel the energy from the Moon. You will want to cast this spell outside.

Gather your ingredients—you will need a glass and a bowl, sugar, water, a single currency bill, and the Full Moon.

Set up your altar somewhere where the Moon can reach it—either outside or in a large window. Take your bowl, preferably glass, and add a splash of water to it before placing it on a table. Then, add a single spoonful of sugar to the small glass that you also have. DO NOT MIX THE SUGAR AND WATER.

At this point, take the small glass and place it gently into the bowl of water, without getting the water into the glass. Then, carefully place the bill underneath the bowl, taking care to not spill any ingredients. As you do this, say:

"Brilliant Moon, may your light be transferred and may your radiance extend to my financial situation.
May the water be the mirror, the sugar, the conductor, and allow Abundance to flood into all areas of my existence.
Dear, Moon, you have my deepest gratitude, because you are always listening."

Now, leave the bowl out overnight and take it in first thing in the morning, before the sun has had a chance to shine on it. At this point, take out the bill and use it as an amulet, holding it in your wallet and then mix the water and sugar and pour it into the ground.

Casting Spell During The Waning Gibbous And Last Quarter Moon

Three days after the Full Moon until 7 days later, the Moon is in the Waning Gibbous stage—it still looks swollen, but it is starting to narrow and fade away. This phase of the moon is perfect for eliminating or banishing negativity, bathing spells, spiritual cleanses, and protection spells.

During the Last Quarter Moon, the Moon is making her descent to rest, and so should you. During this period, you should try to avoid engaging in much magic, instead choosing to remove yourself from any negative behaviors. The only magic that is usually used during this time consists of justice spells.

Banish All Evil

This spell is intended to protect you from any negativity, allowing you to eliminate a curse, or avoid being stuck in a home with negative feelings.

When you use this spell, you are making yourself less vulnerable, eliminating that evil from your environment.

For this spell, you will need an apple, a bay leaf, a knife, and a cutting board. You will start with the apple, a symbol of purity and rebirth, as well as the communication with the Other World. Along with the bay leaf, which is used as an offering, the apple will be used together, creating a perfect combination between the two that will help you purify. This spell is best done on a Friday if you can.

Start by placing your apple onto an altar or a table and look at it, focus on imbuing it with your intentions and your goal—clearing the room from negativity. Now, imagine that you are creating a shield around you, protecting you so any negativity bounces right off of you. As you do this, holding the image in your mind, slice the apple in half, leaving both sitting face-up on the table. Place the bay leaf on top of one piece of the apple while saying:

This should be repeated at least three times, loudly and firmly as you do so. When you do this, believing that your wish will be granted, you will see the universe answer accordingly. When you are done, place the apple back together and bury it in the yard.

Cord Cutting Spell

This spell is all about meditation and healing, allowing you to remove energy bonds that are no longer important for you. They allow you to slice the relationship between two people, freeing you from a bad relationship or if you have come to realize that too much negative energy is being bounced back and forth. This works because you are literally cutting the cord between yourself and another person, stopping that intimate energetic bond altogether.

You will need a single white candle, an athame, and a lighter or a match. Start first by lighting your candle in front of you while you sit. Close your eyes and let your mind fall into a state of mindfulness. As this happens, allow your mind to visualize where you connect to the other person. Do you attack at the hands? The heads? The heart? These parts can vary greatly, but they are important to identify. Identify the sources and points of connection. Then, open your eyes, and using your athame, or your finger if you do not have one, slowly and deliberately slice in a circle around yourself, creating a full circle and repeating:

"I remove this energy from myself.
I reject and release the cords for my greater welfare.
I forgive and release myself."

As you do this, turn around again, imagining how you have sliced away any of the cords and imagining how they have all faded away into oblivion. As they melt, imagine positive light energy healing you and the wounds you have created.

Release Spell

Sometimes, it is far too easy to get caught up on someone who you are better off without. Luckily for you, there is a spell for that! This spell will help you release anyone who has hurt you or that you simply cannot forget. You can finally break those ties with this spell, allowing yourself to be free at last. This spell works because of the affirmation, aligned with the ritual, create your intention to really engage in making big changes.

All you will need for this spell is a paper and pen—write down the name of the person you wish to forget. Fold the paper as much as you can, and with each fold, allow your mind to empty and ask yourself to let go of the other person forever. As you do so, repeat:

"I free you and I declare,
This is the best for us everywhere."

After reciting this, take the paper and place it underneath the threshold for your front door, and the next morning, take the paper away from your home, leaving it far away from your home. Try burying it into a garden or next to a crossroad if you wanted to get symbolic.

Return to Sender Spell

This spell is a way to get karmic justice—basically, you are promoting any and all karmic retribution in the hope that the other person gets what he or she deserves and you did not do anything that will obviously link you to the other person.

This spell works because you are essentially using a black candle to create a mirror—anything that the other person has done to you simply bounces back toward them, and you sue a lemon and cloves to protect and cleanse yourself, while also using the lemon to purify the air and absorb the negativity.

Gather your tools—a black candle, a lemon, a knife, incense, and cloves, and light your incense. Think of whatever has happened to you recently—anything that has been negative, and it does not matter who caused what or why things played out how they did. Focus on your feelings and acknowledge them. Then, light your candle and slice the lemon.

Take the cloves, placing three pieces inside one half and then do the same with the other half. As you do this, repeat:

"The harm you inflicted is now your own.
Retribution is here, I am not alone."

Once more, imagine what you think justice would encompass and then imagine that image leaving into the universe. Blow the candle and release your intentions.

Circle of Protection

Your circle of protection spell will involve several quick and easy steps, but when you master this process, you can ensure that you are able to remain protected as you cast other spells as well. Keep in mind that everyone chooses different methods to cast their spells, and because of that, you should feel free to experiment and really figure out what works best for you.

First, you must identify the space that you will need—if you need significant space, you need a significant circle, which of course, means significant energy output. Make sure that you bring everything into your circle before you begin to cast it, enabling you to avoid ending the circle halfway through it in order to go fetch whatever you have forgotten. If you do need to exit the circle at any point however, you can always make it a point to visualize a small door that you use to enter and exit rather than dismantling the whole thing.

Then, clean your ritual area—using salt and a broom, you can purify your space. Burn some sage if you think it could be useful as well, and then draw the circle around the space that you are using. Some people do this with an outline in their minds, tracing the circle with their finger while other people make a physical circle. As you create the circle, make sure that you visualize the energy protecting and shielding you for harm.

With your circle formed, you are then free to line it with any elemental objects if you will need them. If not, you are ready to finish any other spells that you have to get through.

Casting Spell During The Waning Crescent Moon

The last phase of the moon, the waning crescent, is the ending of the cycle. At this point, you should look back at what has happened through the cycle, either acknowledging anything you did well or recognizing any mistakes that were problematic and kept your intentions from coming true. At this stage, you should focus primarily on spells and rituals for rest and gratitude as you rest and reflect back on your last Lunar Cycle.

Anti-Evil Offering

One particular form of this is the anti-evil offering, which appeals to Bast, an Egyptian Goddess who protected the home. She was responsible for joy of life, as well as harmony. She is primarily seen as a woman with a cat head, carrying a musical instrument, and she is considered the solar goddess.

This spell is more of a ritual, honoring the great Goddess Bast, offering her incense and offerings of chocolate, feathers, sunflowers, honey, or milk. Offer her a genuine prayer of thanks, recognizing that she is powerful. Create an offering to her and write a devotional text, thanking her for how the birth of the Gods and her creation of the world around you. Recognize and thank her for clearing evil from your life, expelling the evil from within you and freeing you from negativity once and for all.

Hestia Offering

For Hestia, the Goddess of the home and family, presiding over the hearth and the very heart of the home, you should light a purple candle when honoring and reflecting upon her contribution to the world around you. Light an incense of rosemary, juniper, or lavender, and create an offering to her— most often, something sweet or a portion a family meal will leave her quite pleased, as would bread or a sweet wine of some sort.

When you are able to pray to Hestia, devoting yourself to worshipping her, you can use her energy to banish any negativity that goes your way, threatening the structure of the very family home that she represents.

Just as with Bast, try to honor Hestia, creating a prayer to her and thanking her for her support and aid. Appeal to her to banish any sadness from your home, and ask for her to allow you to bathe in good fortune once and for all, drawing on her love and mercy.

Gratitude Spell

Finally, the last spell that you will encounter in this book is the Gratitude Spell. This spell involves one candle, rose petals and salt in order to evoke gratitude and good luck. In this spell, you will surround a dish that is placed upon your altar with salt, creating a circle. Then, you add the petals to the top of the salt. In the center of the dish, place the white candle and light it. Breathe and visualize your own gratitude in the world.

As you do this, recite:

"Only gratitude and positive energy flows from me right now."

In doing so, you return your gratitude to the outside world, and you can then sit and meditate for a few moments, focusing on how you would like to see your intentions and good energy waves returned to you in time.

You will repeat this ritual several times for one week with the same ingredients, and on the seventh day, you should allow the candle to burn out.

Conclusion

Thank you for making it through to the end of *Wicca Moon Magic!* Hopefully, you found plenty of useful information as you read this book. You were guided through so much information about the Goddess, the Moon, and the energy she puts out into the world as she transforms from the newborn Infant to the Maiden, eager to live and grow, to the loving, benevolent, comforting Mother, all the way to the elderly Crone, wise and fair before the cycle begins once more.

This cycle of life is something that is visible everywhere, but there is beauty in that—there is beauty in the cycle and in the idea that everyone ends where they began, only to start the process over again. In death, space is made for life, and that is a primary principle when you are using Wiccan magic. You will see that this magic is quite cyclical—good intentions go out, and other intentions and energy have to fill its place. This can be perturbing to some, but it is actually quite poetic and beautiful—with every intention that you send out, freeing your energy back into the universe, you make room for something else, and that something else may be what you have always been hoping for.

With the knowledge you have acquired during your time reading this book, you have learned so much information—you have discovered the intimate relationship between the Moon and everything on Earth, ranging from the ocean tides to the shape of the atmosphere, and quite probably, much of human nature itself. You have learned about how the Moon's power can be harnessed in several ways, including how to garden and how to act accordingly with the tides and how they may impact your life. You learned about charging your items under the Moon and of creating and using Moon Water. You learned how to tap into your intuition with the help of the great, beautiful Moon and how-to live-in honor of her.

With all of this information about Lunar Rhythms, Cycles, magic, and spells, you are now ready to make a pivotal decision in your life—is Wicca magic something you desire to practice? This book was absolutely an introduction to the concept of Wicca magic in regards to the Moon. If this is something that has resonated with you, it may be time to continue your research and begin gathering your tools that you will need to use. If you are not yet sure, you may decide to pick up some new topics to study instead. If this book just didn't do it for you, or you are too dubious to believe in the beauty of the Moon's magic and the Universe's energy, that is okay, too. Ultimately, you must make the decision yourself.

Lastly, if this book was useful to you at all, please do not hesitate to leave a review on Amazon! Your feedback is always greatly appreciated!

Recommendations For Further Reading

Even as this book draws to a close, it is important to point you in the right direction to develop a stronger foundation on what Wicca really means to those who practice it. If you have decided that Wicca is appealing to you, that is fantastic! From here, you may be interested in studying crystal magic, herbs, candle magic, and more, and this section will provide you with a handful of websites that you may find particularly useful as you continue your journey.

Particularly if you are interested in meeting and speaking with others who share the Wiccan belief, online resources are fantastic. There are plenty of online communities in which people utilize forums to communicate with other Wiccan witches.

For example, Reddit's Wicca board may offer you plenty of insight:

https://www.reddit.com/r/Wicca/

or you may find benefit in reading over a forum known as Everything Under the Moon—and they are not kidding. There are so many discussions of everything from Books of Shadows, Kitchen Magick, understanding nature spirits, astrology, and, well, everything under the Moon.

http://everythingunderthemoon.net/forum/

Perhaps one of the most straightforward websites that you can go to for future information is The Celtic Connection, simply known as wicca.com.

https://wicca.com/

If you would prefer books for further reading, just type in "Wicca magic" on Kindle Unlimited and you are bound to find dozens of results readily available as well.

Sacred Symbols You Need To Know

As one final note before this book wraps to a close, you need to understand several of the sacred symbols—these symbols will pop up again and again in Wiccan magic, so the sooner you get to know them, the better.

Air

One of the classical elements used in the Wiccan ritual, air is the Eastern element. This is viewed as the breath of life itself and is most commonly a triangle with a solid horizontal line parallel to the base.

Ankh

This is an Egyptian symbol, but it has still made its way into Wiccan practice. This is the symbol for eternal life and represents the key to life itself, with the topmost loop representing the sun, the horizontal line representing femininity and the vertical bar representing masculine energy.

Celtic Shield Knot

This is a sign for protection—this knot is meant to tie together fire, water, earth, and air in each of the four corners.

Earth

One of the four classical elements, Earth is a triangle with the tip pointing downward, with a horizontal line parallel to the flat top, creating the mirrored image of the sign of air. It is the ultimate feminine symbol, relevant to spring and the Mother.

Eye of Horus

Another Egyptian symbol was used to represent healing and protection.

Eye of Ra

Yet another Egyptian symbol, this symbol represented the Sun god and was also a sign of protection, much like the Eye of Horus—it was regularly painted upon boats to protect them.

Fire

The third of the four classical elements, fire is masculine and purifying. It destroys, and yet creates at the same time. This is a triangle with the point upwards with no lines inside of it.

Hecate's Wheel

This is not a constant in Wicca—some will utilize this symbol, representing the Triple Goddess's forms, but others choose to forego it altogether.

The Horned God

Representing the ultimate masculine energy, the Horned God is used to invoke the God during rituals.

Pentacle

This particular symbol is widely recognized—the five-pointed star within a circle. It contains the four elements of air, fire, earth, and water, with the fifth point either representing the self or the spiritual energy. This is potentially linked back to the slicing of an apple crossways, in which you sever the top from the bottom rather than cutting it down the middle along the core—you see a five-pointed star within the circle of the apple.

Seax-Wica

Not commonly worshipped or used, this symbol represents the sun (the circle), the moon (the crescent), and the eight Sabbats in the center.

Solar Cross

This represents the sun as well as the cyclical nature of the elements and seasons. It is usually created as a circle with two parallel lines going up and down the diameter, and then two more parallel lines running across the diameter horizontally, and a circle in the center where the four lines create a smaller square.

Sun Wheel

This sign represents the Wheel of the Year—showing a circle with eight slices through it. It is linked to masculinity.

Thor's Hammer

Although this is particularly found within Norse Pagan traditions, it can also be found elsewhere. It shows a power over the sky—particularly over thunder and lighting.

Triple Horn of Odin

This image is created by three drinking horns that have been interlocked together, representing Odin, who is the father of the Norse gods. It shares both masculine and feminine aspects.

Triple Moon

This is a full moon in the center, plus a waxing and waning crescent moon on either side, representing the Maiden, Mother, and Crone.

Triple Spiral

This is a Celtic design that is occasionally found within Buddhist writing—it is used to represent the earth, sea, and sky.

Triquetra

The Triquetra is an image in which three points have overlapped, but it is rarely found on its own— usually, it was just a filler symbol to avoid blank space.

Water

One of the four classical elements, water is feminine and related to the Goddess. It is the inverted triangle, directly associated with the shape of the womb.

Yin Yang

This particular symbol is primarily Eastern rather than found in most modern Wiccan or Pagan sources, but it can be found in various places throughout the world, thanks to its ability to represent a perfect balance to two opposites. It can be used to invoke balance and rebirth.

www.ingramcontent.com/pod-product-compliance
Lightning Source LLC
LaVergne TN
LVHW011009200726
843509LV00011B/1027